DECLASSIFYING
9/11

A Between The Lines And Behind The Scenes Look At The September 11 Attacks

Aidan Monaghan

iUniverse, Inc.
Bloomington

DECLASSIFYING 9/11
A Between The Lines And Behind The Scenes Look At The September 11 Attacks

iUniverse books may be ordered through booksellers or by contacting:

iUniverse
1663 Liberty Drive
Bloomington, IN 47403
www.iuniverse.com
1-800-Authors (1-800-288-4677)

ISBN: 978-1-4759-2022-2 (sc)
ISBN: 978-1-4759-2028-4 (ebk)

Printed in the United States of America

iUniverse rev. date: 04/30/2013

Contents

Introduction

With the passage of a decade since the events of September 11, 2001, the mostly unspecific and essentially unproven allegations made by major corporate media outlets and the U.S. federal government regarding what reportedly unfolded that day, have not held up well under scrutiny. They would include views supported only by limited and unverified circumstantial evidence that religious extremists with little piloting experience hijacked and piloted sophisticated aircraft into major U.S. buildings, ultimately leading to the complete physics-defying destructions of most of them.

Also alleged by U.S. federal and industry experts with little supporting evidence, is that office fires, limited structural damage and simple gravity, caused three superbly built World Trade Center (WTC) skyscrapers to collapse entirely to the ground. Comprehensively reported here is the fact that official documentation regarding details of activity within the WTC buildings just prior to September 11, 2001 has largely been reported as destroyed, absent or exempt from disclosure under federal and local Freedom of Information (FOI) laws. Unavailable records for major WTC construction and renovation projects underway just prior to and until September 11, 2001 are made all the more interesting in light of scientific evidence establishing the substantial presence of high-tech explosive incendiaries recovered from the destroyed contents of the WTC buildings.

The evidence for the presence and even use of explosives at the WTC on September 11 is substantial and growing. Dozens of on scene emergency responders and survivors reported major explosions throughout the WTC complex just prior to the destructions of both WTC towers [1,2]. The federal government's own analysis of just the little structural steel from the WTC site that was not quickly destroyed by authorities, exhibits the effects reportedly related to such incendiaries. These effects would include sulfidation, extreme erosion and even evaporation of this steel [3,4]. Live September 11 television broadcasts captured what appeared to be such incendiary molten material already ignited and emanating from one of the WTC tower plane impact floors moments before the building's unexpected collapse [5]. The presence within the later collapsed WTC wreckage of such molten material was later even documented by multiple credible sources [6]. Moreover, the types of white plumes of aluminum oxide material associated with the ignition of thermite were also observed emanating from the WTC towers before and during each of their collapses [7].

Were the said construction projects linked to the presence of these explosive incendiaries and thus the WTC's destruction? Was the WTC construction contractor performing the said construction connected in any way to the federal agency who was the leading developer of such materials circa 2001? Was there any association between this construction contractor's then CEO and then U.S. President George W. Bush, whose pre-September 11 middle-east war ambitions were later facilitated by the attacks?

What happened to the 3,000+ Securities and Exchange Commission (SEC) investigative files regarding suspect Wall Street activities that were stored within the offices of the collapsed WTC building 7, which was not hit by an airplane on September 11 and whose extraordinary collapse rate was measured to be at free-fall speed? And what is known of the Department of Defense (DoD) and Central Intelligence Agency (CIA) tenants of this building? These questions and others will be answered by FOI replies from relevant local and federal agencies, obtained by the author and presented here.

Also reported here in detail, is seldom discussed remotely controlled and automated aviation industry technology researched by the author, that was intensively developed by the U.S. federal government and commercial aviation industry just prior to September 11, 2001, that made the observed aircraft attacks entirely possible without the control of human hijacker pilots, raising the real possibility of alternative explanations for what unfolded that day in the skies over America. Is there evidence that the September 11 aircraft attacks were timed to coincide with brief periods of superior and newly available aviation guidance Global Positioning System (GPS) service, which is relied upon by aircraft autopilot systems? Has the limited September 11 aircraft activity information surrendered by authorities, been found to be in conflict with information available publicly on other federal government websites? What are the reasons that make the September 11 aircraft "black box" information suspect and unreliable? Such "black box" data is in fact, the most relied upon evidence of alleged September 11 flight hijacker takeovers.

Although other circumstantial happenings have been relied upon to support official hijacker flight takeover claims, these events are shown to be unproven and without other corroborating evidence. These alleged happenings would include reported flight deck voice transmissions by the accused following their alleged flight deck takeovers and also flight attendant seatback phone calls from the September 11 flight passenger cabins. Yet the said flight deck radio communications are impossible to link to any September 11 flight due to technology limitations and invoices for some alleged flight attendant in-flight phone calls apparently don't exist while others have simply never been produced by authorities [8]. This work will examine these and other important questions.

And what of official claims that accused September 11 hijackers manually deactivated aircraft transponders, making the identifying and performance information for these aircraft invisible to Air Traffic Control (ATC) and thus making them purportedly more difficult for air defense systems to locate and defend against? September 11 flight transponder deactivations were central evidence cited in support of alleged flight deck takeovers by the accused, but is there in fact any evidence supporting claims that accused hijackers actually deactivated these transponders manually, apart from the simple loss of flight transponder signal information? And were there other means circa 2001 for causing such aircraft radar information to vanish from ATC screens? Was any such transponder signal blocking capability limited to only military aircraft?

If so, the implications raised by the presence of aerial U.S. military war-games underway on the morning of September 11, as well as the confirmed deployment of the U.S. Air Force's E-4B aerial communications platform within the general proximity of all four September 11 flights, are noteworthy.

Could September 11 flight transponder signal losses have in fact jeopardized the alleged plot of those accused of hijacking these flights? Is there evidence that the journey into the WTC by the only September 11 flight with a continuously active but altered transponder signal, was actually facilitated in ways that the other flights with inactive transponders were not?

From within minutes of the reported impact of American Airlines flight 77 (AA 77) with the Pentagon building in Arlington, Virginia on September 11, 2001, intense public speculation about what precisely unfolded upon the property of the military headquarters of the United States has continued to this day.

Although certain alleged events there may be a settled matter for the federal government and mainstream media, their earliest responses to the catastrophe had in fact contributed to the seeming mystery.

In 2006, determined amateur researchers were able to record the on-scene recollections of some of the few individuals who actually witnessed most of what unfolded on September 11, 2001 while just outside of the Pentagon. And while certain unconfirmed conclusions drawn from these accounts have become a matter of separate controversy, these accounts may also have provided the circumstantial evidence leading one to less obvious but perhaps the most plausible and remarkable of all possible event outcomes.

Examined here in detail are the descriptions by members of law enforcement and employees of other properties just adjacent to the Pentagon, who describe the final seconds of flight for an American Airlines Boeing 757 as they witnessed it while en route to the Pentagon. While at first these accounts seem consistent with official versions of events, upon closer examination they are seemingly fatal to official allegations and other purported circumstantial evidence for less than obvious reasons. And if so, what could possibly be the motive for misleading the public about what appears to be a less than consequential flight path discrepancy for AA 77 during its final seconds of flight? Were parts of the September 11 Pentagon crash scene altered to allow for the introduction of false evidence that later became central to the federal government's official event hypothesis? All of these questions will be examined here in detail, based largely on original research, relevant federal Freedom of Information records obtained by the author and through intensive examinations of the said events.

1. Buildings Without Paper Trails

During the half-decade prior to September 11, 2001, WTC buildings 1, 2 and 7 were subject to major renovations ranging from the creation of a New York City Office of Emergency Management (OEM) "bunker" within WTC 7, to modernizations of elevators within WTC 1 and 2 that qualified as among the largest ever. Were these renovations related in any way to the subsequent and unprecedented destructions of each building?

WTC 7 was also home to branch offices of the Central Intelligence Agency (CIA), the Securities, Exchange Commission (SEC) and the Department of Defense (DoD).

Curiously, local and federal agency records regarding the intensive renovation work just before September 11 within these buildings, have either been reported as destroyed as a result of the September 11 attacks while in storage upon WTC property, been declared exempt from disclosure or as being nonexistent. Surprisingly, such records would include those for some of the most extensive construction and renovation projects in the industry on record, underway within WTC buildings 1 and 2 during the months, days and even hours before the September 11 attacks, including substantial work occurring within building elevator shafts. As will be seen, access to such work spaces is strictly limited to only select personnel per federal regulations.

I Port Authority of NY/NJ: Records for Reported WTC Renovation Work Destroyed on 9/11

Turner Construction company, who supervised the 2000 demolition of the Seattle Kingdome, participated in the post-September 11 Ground Zero clean-up and performed extensive renovations within the WTC towers just prior to September 11, was also coincidentally or not, performing unspecified renovation work throughout the WTC complex until the very morning of September 11, 2001.

> Terror devastates A/E/C firms: 12 employees of Turner Construction were located in an office in the third subbasement of Tower 1, the north tower. Turner had been performing renovation work in various parts of the center and had occupied various office spaces.[1]

The Port Authority of NY/NJ reported via an April 2009 FOI response that records describing such work or other projects were destroyed on September 11, 2001, presumably as a result of being stored within one or more WTC buildings. A December 2000 WTC property assessment described required renovation work to be completed within one year, upon supportive steel columns within elevator shafts of WTC towers 1 and 2 that was immediately pending or already underway. The Merritt and Harris "Due Diligence Physical Condition Survey" report of the WTC property condition dated December, 2000, noted rusting of major steel columns within elevator shafts of both WTC 1 and WTC 2. The report's authors recommended corrective action to be completed within one year of the report's date.[2]

1

THE PORT AUTHORITY OF NY & NJ

Kathleen P. Bincoletto
FOI Administrator

April 8, 2009

Mr. Aidan Monaghan
███████████████
Las Vegas, NV ██████

Re: Freedom of Information Reference No. 11130

Dear Mr. Monaghan:

This is a response to your request dated today, which has been processed under the Port Authority's policy on Freedom of Information (the "Policy," copy enclosed) for "copies of records, contracts or a bibliography of contracts, pertaining to Turner Construction Company, prior to January, 2002."

Please be advised that Port Authority records that may have been responsive to your request were destroyed at the World Trade Center on September 11, 2001.

Sincerely,

Kathleen P. Bincoletto

Kathleen P. Bincoletto
FOI Administrator

Enclosure

225 Park Avenue South
New York, NY 10003
T: 212 435 2542 F: 212 435 7555

kbincoletto@panynj.gov

Port Authority of New York and New Jersey Correspondence (2009)

The Indian Head Naval Surface Warfare Center (IHNSWC), a laboratory managed by the Naval Sea Systems Command (NAVSEA), was described during the 1990s as the "National Center for Energetics"[3], the "Pentagon's jargon to broadly describe explosive materials, propellants and pyrotechnics" and as the "only reliable source of aluminum nano-powders in the United States".

Aluminum nano-powders are a major component of the nano-thermitic explosive incendiaries later discovered within dust samples created by the collapses of the WTC towers.[4]

It has been learned that developers of nano-thermite had designed a form of nano-thermite circa 2000 that can be painted onto surfaces and is very resistant to premature or unintended ignition. Other NAVSEA divisions are also known to develop paintable nano-scale corrosion protectant coatings. It remains unknown what entity provided the corrosion protection materials presumably used upon the major steel supportive columns within the elevator shafts of WTC 1 and 2, during the nine month period just before the September 11 attacks as called for. An examination of Turner Construction's published capabilities suggests that specialized work is to some extent delegated to construction sub-contractors operating under Turner direction.

In 1997 Turner Construction also constructed the new headquarters for NAVSEA.

> During 1997, the company completed work on . . . the Naval Sea Systems Command Headquarters (NAVSEA) for the Navy in Washington, DC. [5]

IHNSWC advised via a 2012 FOIA reply that they possess no records regarding uses for nano-thermite, even though by 2008 IHNSWC was the leading developer of nano-thermite.[6]

In addition to Turner Construction's documented construction and worksite materials collection and disposal capabilities, such as those utilized after September 11 at the WTC site, they interestingly are also expert at the management of major structure demolition. However, such capability only seems to be in evidence during the controlled demolition of the Seattle Kingdome during March of 2000, just 18 months before September 11, 2001. In fact, this controlled demolition is recognized as a Guinness World Record for the controlled implosion of the largest building by volume.[7]

> Is Dome's demise a date with fate?

> Saturday, March 4, 2000

> SEATTLE POST-INTELLIGENCER REPORTER

> Mark your calendar. The day of the Kingdome's demise—March 26—is drawing near. "The roof will look like choreography (as it collapses)," explained Thomas Gerlach of Turner Construction, the company overseeing the demolition.[8]

DEPARTMENT OF THE NAVY
NAVAL SURFACE WARFARE CENTER
INDIAN HEAD DIVISION
3767 STRAUSS AVENUE
SUITE 201
INDIAN HEAD, MD 20640-5190

5720
Ser CE1/026

Mr. Aidan Monaghan

MAR 1 6 2012

Las Vegas, NV

Dear Mr. Monaghan:

    This is a final response to FOIA request number 2012F0200008
in which you seek records describing all uses or applications of
Naval Surface Warfare Center, Indian Head Division nano-thermite
products.

    We have conducted an extensive search of our records and
have not found any records responsive to your specific request.

    If you have any questions please contact Mrs. Kelly Carey,
our FOIA Director. She can be reached at 301-744-6739 or
Kelly.carey@navy.mil.

                                    Sincerely,

                                    A. BUDUO III
                                    Captain, U.S. Navy
                                    Commander

United States Naval Surface Warfare Center Correspondence (2012)

Work previous to the September 11 attacks performed by Turner Construction at the WTC included reported fireproofing of the only WTC tower floors that interestingly were also struck by United and American airlines flights on September 11, 2001 and that later burned and "failed".[9]

The immediate renovation work recommended by the Merritt and Harris WTC property assessment, upon steel columns contained within elevator shafts of both WTC towers [10], is governed by the Occupational Safety Hazard Administration (OSHA) and is deemed to be "confined spaces" activity, which implies an isolated work environment and restricted location access. OSHA has advised via FOIA reply that no records for such WTC workspace permits could be located that could reveal what work was being performed there and by whom.

Turner Construction also reportedly occupied the 38th floor of WTC 1. The Port Authority of NY/NJ claims that contracts with Turner Construction—including those that might describe the renovation work being performed by Turner Construction until the very morning of September 11, 2001—were also destroyed that day.

As noted, Turner Construction later participated in the collection and disposal of the steel wreckage of the WTC towers following September 11, 2001:

> Australia's Lend Lease has secured the contract to manage the clean-up operation at New York's World Trade Center site . . . will also be in charge of AMEC Construction Management, Turner Construction and Tully Construction, which have been contracted to work on the site. [11]

The CEO for Turner Construction Company on September 11, 2001 and appointed in 1999, was Tom Leppert [12]. Leppert joined the board of Turner in 1998, was subsequently elected mayor of Dallas, Texas, is currently a candidate for the U.S. Senate for the state of Texas and interestingly has ties with former president George W. Bush and Carlos M. Gutierrez, Secretary of the U.S. Department of Commerce (DoC). The National Institute of Standards and Technology (NIST), a bureau of the DoC, was also interestingly assigned to investigate the collapses of WTC 1, 2 and 7 during Gutierrez' tenure at the DoC.

> PRESIDENTIAL APPOINTMENT FOR MAYOR LEPPERT: President George W. Bush appointed Dallas Mayor Tom Leppert to the President's Commission on White House Fellows. [13]

> Mayor Leppert meets with Bush—Dallas Business Journal: Dallas Mayor Tom Leppert, along with a group of 11 other mayors, met with President George W. Bush and Commerce Secretary Carlos M. Gutierrez Wednesday at the White House to discuss a free trade agreement with the South American countries of Peru and Colombia. [14]

II NYC Department of Buildings: WTC Buildings 1, 2 and 7 Deemed "Sensitive Buildings", Plans Exempt from Disclosure

Within a September 13, 2011 FOI response from the New York City Department of Buildings (DoB), it was reported that WTC buildings 1, 2 and 7 have been deemed "sensitive" buildings and thus, plans for these buildings have been exempted from public disclosure by statute. Mysteriously, "if disclosed, the documents requested would endanger the life or safety of any person." No public safety basis for the exemption declaration was provided.

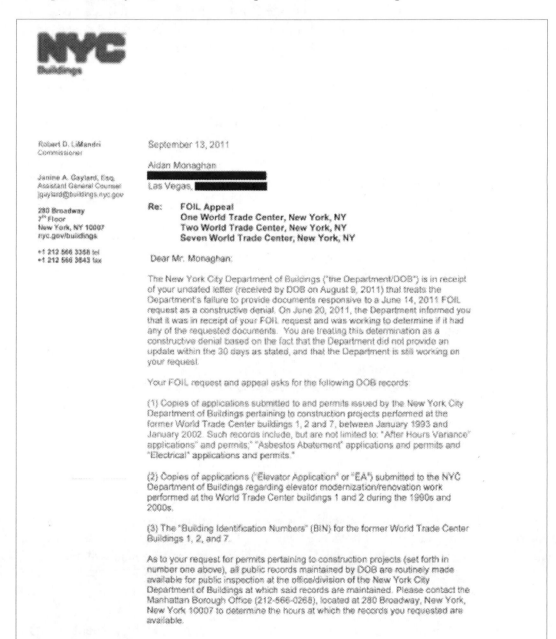

Robert D. LiMandri
Commissioner

Janine A. Gaylard, Esq.
Assistant General Counsel
jgaylard@buildings.nyc.gov

280 Broadway
7th Floor
New York, NY 10007
nyc.gov/buildings

+1 212 566 3358 tel
+1 212 566 3843 fax

September 13, 2011

Aidan Monaghan

Las Vegas,

Re: FOIL Appeal
        One World Trade Center, New York, NY
        Two World Trade Center, New York, NY
        Seven World Trade Center, New York, NY

Dear Mr. Monaghan:

The New York City Department of Buildings ("the Department/DOB") is in receipt of your undated letter (received by DOB on August 9, 2011) that treats the Department's failure to provide documents responsive to a June 14, 2011 FOIL request as a constructive denial. On June 20, 2011, the Department informed you that it was in receipt of your FOIL request and was working to determine if it had any of the requested documents. You are treating this determination as a constructive denial based on the fact that the Department did not provide an update within the 30 days as stated, and that the Department is still working on your request.

Your FOIL request and appeal asks for the following DOB records:

(1) Copies of applications submitted to and permits issued by the New York City Department of Buildings pertaining to construction projects performed at the former World Trade Center buildings 1, 2 and 7, between January 1993 and January 2002. Such records include, but are not limited to: "After Hours Variance" applications" and permits;" "Asbestos Abatement" applications and permits and "Electrical" applications and permits."

(2) Copies of applications ("Elevator Application" or "EA") submitted to the NYC Department of Buildings regarding elevator modernization/renovation work performed at the World Trade Center buildings 1 and 2 during the 1990s and 2000s.

(3) The "Building Identification Numbers" (BIN) for the former World Trade Center Buildings 1, 2, and 7.

As to your request for permits pertaining to construction projects (set forth in number one above), all public records maintained by DOB are routinely made available for public inspection at the office/division of the New York City Department of Buildings at which said records are maintained. Please contact the Manhattan Borough Office (212-566-0268), located at 280 Broadway, New York, New York 10007 to determine the hours at which the records you requested are available.

build safe | live safe

New York City Department of Buildings Correspondence (2011)

I am told that Asbestos Abatement" applications are filed with the New York City Department of Environmental Protection ("DEP"), so the Department would not have any responsive records. Please direct your request for these records to DEP.

As to request number 2, BIS shows no elevator records during the time period requested.

As to request number 3, I am advised by the Director of Application Support that our system is not able to provide BIN information by dates. Since there is no record containing this information, your request is for information that is not properly a FOIL request, since FOIL applies only to existing records.

Please keep in mind that since the Port Authority of New York is not under DOB jurisdiction, it may not have filed with DOB for work undertaken at the above reference properties.

Also, please note that 1, 2 and 7 World Trade Center have been designated as "sensitive buildings." Pursuant to 87(2) (f) of the Public Officer's Law, plans for sensitive buildings are not released under FOIL, on the grounds that, "if disclosed, the documents requested would endanger the life or safety of any person."

This constitutes the Department's final determination.

Sincerely,

Janine A. Gaylard
Assistant General Counsel/Records Appeals Officer

cc: Juliet Neisser, Associate General Counsel
     Angela Orridge, Records Access Officer
     Robert Freeman, Committee on Open Government, Dept. of State

Interestingly, the DoB reply also advised that the Port Authority of NY/NJ are not under the jurisdiction of the NYC DoB and that records for major pre-September 11 WTC renovations undertaken by the Port Authority of NY/NJ may not have been submitted to the DoB.

Dear Mr. Monaghan:

The New York City Department of Buildings ("the Department/DOB") is in receipt of your undated letter (received by DOB on August 9, 2011) that treats the Department's failure to provide documents responsive to a June 14, 2011 FOIL request as a constructive denial. On June 20, 2011, the Department informed you that it was in receipt of your FOIL request and was working to determine if it had any of the requested documents.

Your FOIL request and appeal asks for the following DOB records:

Copies of applications submitted to and permits issued by the New York City Department of Buildings pertaining to construction projects performed at the former World Trade Center buildings 1, 2 and 7, between January 1993 and January 2002. Such records include, but are not limited to:

(1) "After Hours Variance" applications and permits; "Asbestos Abatement" applications and permits and "Electrical" applications and permits."

(2) Copies of applications ("Elevator Application" or "EA") submitted to the NYC Department of Buildings regarding elevator modernization/renovation work performed at the World Trade Center buildings 1 and 2 during the 1990s and 2000s.

Please keep in mind that since the Port Authority of New York is not under DOB jurisdiction, it may not have filed with DOB for work undertaken at the above referenced properties.

Also, please note that 1, 2 and 7 World Trade Center have been designated as "sensitive buildings". Pursuant to 87(2) (f) of the Public Officer's Law, plans for sensitive buildings are not released under FOIL, on the grounds that, "if disclosed, the documents requested would endanger the life or safety of any person."

This constitutes the Department's final determination.

Sincerely,

Janine A Gaylord

Assistant General Counsel/Records Appeals Officer

III NYC Department of Buildings: No Records for Pre-9/11 WTC Elevator Rebuild, One of the "Largest, Most Sophisticated" Ever

The New York City DoB also reported within a June 6, 2011 FOI response that mysteriously, no records could be located regarding a request for information pertaining to the massive elevator modernization project underway at WTC buildings 1 and 2 until the very morning of September 11, 2001, one of the largest ever. [15]

The DoB governs elevator construction and use within New York City.

The DoB's June 6, 2011 FOI answer reads as follows:

BIS shows no elevator records for the time period in question.

The DoB's Building Information System (BIS) "is the Department of Buildings' main database.

The database was put into production in 1984 and supports Department functions with respect to:

. . . Application Processing (application submission . . .) [16]

The DoB's description of its role regarding elevator installation and use within New York City:

The Department of Buildings' Elevator Division oversees the use and operation of New York City's elevators. [17]

Such duties include the receipt and issuance of construction applications and permits:

Applications and Permits; New Installations or Major Upgrades; File an Elevator Application (EA) to install a new device or perform a substantial upgrade, alteration, replacement or modernization to an existing device. [18]

The New York City building code regarding elevator construction reads as follows:

SUBCHAPTER 18 ELEVATORS AND CONVEYORS; § [C26-1803.1] 27-1001 Permit required.—No construction, alteration or removal shall be commenced until a written work permit therefor shall have been issued by the commissioner [19]

Robert D. LiMandri
Commissioner

Jerome A. Gaylard, Esq.
Assistant General Counsel
jgaylard@buildings.nyc.gov

280 Broadway
7th Floor
New York, NY 10007
nyc.gov/buildings

+1 212 566 3258 tel
+1 212 566 3843 fax

June 6, 2011

Aidan Monaghan
████████████████████
Las Vegas, NV ██████████

Re: **FOIL Appeal**
        One World Trade Center, New York, NY
        Two World Trade Center, New York, NY

Dear Mr. Monaghan:

The New York City Department of Buildings ("the Department/DOB") is in receipt of your April 15, 2011 letter appealing the Department's February 28, 2011 letter that acknowledged receipt of your FOIL request letter and advised you that it was currently working to determine if it had any of the requested documents. DOB's letter further advised that it would notify you within 30 business days regarding the status of your request. You are treating this determination as a constructive denial based on the fact that the Department did not provide an update within the 30 days as stated, and that the Department is still working on your request.

Your FOIL request asked for the following DOB records:

"Copies of inspections and certifications records issued by the New York City Department of Buildings, pertaining to construction projects performed at the World Trade Center Buildings 1 and 2 between January 2000 and January 2002.

Permits or certifications provided by the NYC Department of Buildings regarding elevator modernization/renovation work performed at the former World Trade Center buildings 1 and 2 during the 1990s and 2000s."

According to the Department's Building Information System ("BIS"), there was a complaint registered on January 11, 2001 at 1 World Trade Center, but the Department did not inspect in view of a lack of jurisdiction. Nor are there records of the Department having inspected 1 World Trade Center during the time period in question for any other reason.

There are no records of complaints filed or inspections conducted at 2 World Trade Center for the period requested.

The Department of Buildings records show no violations issued during that period, so there would be no certification records.

BIS shows no elevator records for the time period in question.

Therefore, the Department has no records responsive to your request.

This constitutes the Department's final determination.

build safe | live safe

New York City Department of Buildings Correspondence (2011)

Dear Mr. Monaghan

The New York City Department of Buildings ("the Department/DOB") is in receipt of your April 15, 2011 letter appealing the Department's February 28, 2011 letter that acknowledged receipt of your FOIL request letter and advised you that it was currently working to determine if it had any of the requested documents. DOB's letter further advised that it would notify you within 30 business days regarding the status of your request. You are treating this determination as a constructive denial based on the fact that the Department did not provide an update within the 30 days as stated, and that the Department is still working on your request.

Your FOIL request asked for the following DOB records:

"Copies of inspections and certifications records issued by the New York City Department of Buildings, pertaining to construction projects performed at the World Trade Center Buildings 1 and 2 between January 2000 and January 2002."

"Permits or certifications provided by the NYC Department of Buildings regarding elevator modernization/renovation work performed at the former World Trade Center buildings 1 and 2 during the 1990s and 2000s."

According to the Department's Building Information System ("BIS"), there was a complaint registered on January 11, 2001 at 1 World Trade Center, but the Department did not inspect in view of a lack of jurisdiction. Nor are there records of the Department having inspected 1 World Trade Center during the time period in question for any other reason. There are no records of complaints filed or inspections conducted at 2 World Trade Center for the period requested. The Department of Buildings records show no violations issued during that period, so there would be no certification records.

BIS shows no elevator records for the time period in question. Therefore, the Department has no records responsive to your request. This constitutes the Department's final determination.

IV SEC: No Records Whatsoever Regarding Destroyed WTC 7 SEC Investigation Files

On January 28, 2009, a FOIA reply was provided by the U.S. Securities and Exchange Commission (SEC), advising that no records were located pertaining to descriptions of files stored within WTC 7 regarding the reported 3,000 to 4,000 SEC investigations of suspect Wall Street activity. Such records were reportedly destroyed on September 11, 2001 following the collapse of WTC 7. These investigations included those related to WorldCom which only months after September 11 became the largest Chapter 11 bankruptcy filer ever. Also reportedly destroyed were 10,000 Equal Employment Opportunity Commission (EEOC) case files located within the EEOC's WTC 7 offices.

From: Aidan Monaghan [mailto:a_monaghan@xxx.xxx]
Sent: Monday, December 08, 2008 10:29 AM
To: Osborne, Sonja
Subject: Re: FOIA Request No. 09-00852

I respectfully request copies of the following SEC records:

A bibliography of, copies of, or other records pertaining to investigation records once stored at the SEC offices once located within floors 11-13, of World Trade Center building 7 in New York City, New York.

UNITED STATES
SECURITIES AND EXCHANGE COMMISSION
STATION PLACE
100 F STREET, NE
WASHINGTON, DC 20549

Office of Freedom of Information
& Privacy Act Operations

Mail Stop 5100   January 28, 2009

Mr. Aidan Monaghan

Las Vegas, NV ▓▓▓▓▓▓▓▓

     Re: Freedom of Information Act (FOIA), 5 U.S.C. § 552
         Request No. 09-01257-FOIA

Dear Mr. Monaghan:

    This letter is our final response to your request dated December 15, 2008, and received in this office on December 16, 2008, for information regarding NYRO World Trade Center Records.

    After consulting with other Commission staff, we did not locate or identify any records pertaining to the SEC investigation records stored at the SEC offices once located within floors 11-13, of World Trade Center building 7 in New York City, New York, as of September 11, 2001.

    If you still have reason to believe that the Commission maintains the type of information you seek, please provide us with additional information, which could prompt another search. Otherwise, we conclude that no responsive information exists and we consider this request to be closed.

    You have the right to appeal the adequacy of our search or finding of no responsive information, to our General Counsel under 5 U.S.C. § 552(a)(6), 17 CFR § 200.80(d)(5) and (6). Your appeal must be in writing, clearly marked "Freedom of Information Act Appeal," and should identify the requested records. The appeal may include facts and authorities you consider appropriate.

United States Securities and Exchange Commission Correspondence (2009)

V WTC 7 CIA Field Office Records Exempt from Disclosure

On November 13, 2008, a FOIA reply was provided by the Central Intelligence Agency (CIA) in response to a request for records regarding descriptions of the CIA field office once located on the 25th floor of WTC 7.

The CIA will neither confirm nor deny the existence of such records per Executive Order 12958.

Central Intelligence Agency

Washington, D.C. 20505

November 13, 2008

Mr. Aidan Monaghan
████████████████████
Las Vegas, NV ████████

Reference: F-2009-00002

Dear Mr. Monaghan:

This is a final response to your 22 September 2008 Freedom of Information Act (FOIA) request, received 1 October 2008 in the office of the Information and Privacy Coordinator, for "records that describe the functions of the CIA field office once located in World Trade Center Building 7 in New York City, New York or any other CIA records regarding this field office."

In accordance with section 3.6(a) of Executive Order 12958, as amended, the CIA can neither confirm nor deny the existence or nonexistence of records responsive to your request. The fact of the existence or nonexistence of requested records is currently and properly classified and is intelligence sources and methods information that is protected from disclosure by section 6 of the CIA Act of 1949, as amended. Therefore, the Agency has denied your request pursuant to FOIA exemptions (b)(1) and (b)(3). I have enclosed an explanation of these exemptions for your reference and retention.

CIA Information and Privacy Coordinator Delores M. Nelson made this decision, which you may appeal to the Agency Release Panel, in my care, within 45 days from the date of this letter. Please include the basis of your appeal.

Sincerely,

Delores M. Nelson
Information and Privacy Coordinator

Enclosure

United States Central Intelligence Agency Correspondence (2008)

VI Port Authority of NY/NJ: No Records for WTC Security Company Linked to Bush Family

On February 5, 2009, the Port Authority of New York and New Jersey reported via FOI response that no records were located regarding the pre-September 11, 2001 WTC security companies tied to Marvin Bush, brother of former U.S. president George W. Bush.

THE PORT AUTHORITY OF NY & NJ

Kathleen P. Bincoletto
FOI Administrator

February 5, 2009

Ms. Aidan Monaghan

Las Vegas, NV ▮▮▮▮▮

Re: Freedom of Information Reference No. 11039

Dear Mr. Monaghan:

This is a response to your request dated February 2, 2009, which has been processed under the Port Authority's policy on Freedom of Information (the "Policy," copy enclosed) for "A bibliography of projects performed by Stratesec aka Securacom, during the duration of its reported contract of $8.3 millon that began in October 1996, for work related to the World Trade Center."

We have searched our files and found no records responsive to your request.

Please refer to the above FOI Reference number in any future correspondence relating to your request.

Sincerely,

Kathleen P. Bincoletto

Kathleen P. Bincoletto
FOI Administrator

Enclosure

Port Authority of New York and New Jersey Correspondence (2009)

The presence of a Bush family influenced security firm known as Stratesec/Securacom upon WTC property was reported by other publications:

> Marvin Bush was reelected to the Stratesec board of directors annually from 1993 through 1999. His last reelection was on May 25, 1999, for July 1999 to June 2000 . . . The company emphasized continuing relationships with a few big long-term clients, including the World Trade Center, home to the Twin Towers.[20]

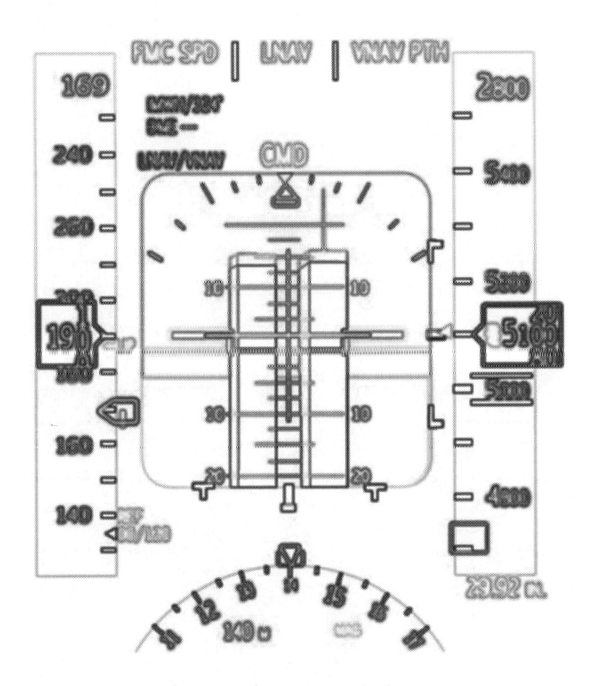

2. Planes Without Paper Trails

It is known that commercial airliners have been utilized at various times by various authorities, for research and development and law enforcement training purposes. As will be shown, research and development flights utilizing loaned commercial Boeing aircraft have even included avionics hardware modifications. Were the four September 11 aircraft ever similarly utilized or even modified in ways that contributed to their performance that day?

Although the reportedly recovered FDR information for AA 77 and UA 93 is capable of containing the final 25 hours of flight data for a given aircraft and therefore the pre-September 11 flight history for each aircraft, federal authorities have been unwilling to provide this specific information, which could be compared to and corroborated by related information already provided by other federal agencies.

Since September 11, 2001, discrepancies regarding the pre-September 11 service history of the four September 11 aircraft have come to light.

FOIA records confirm that the federal agency that monitors commercial aviation flight activity, the Bureau of Transportation Statistics (BTS), have provided two sets of contradictory pre-September 11 historical information for these four aircraft without explanation.

I NTSB Refusal to Provide Converted Pre-September 11 Flight FDR Binary Data

Although the National Transportation Safety Board (NTSB) has provided certain September 11 flight FDR download file information via FOIA release, other binary FDR information has not been converted. Subsequent FOIA appeals of the agency for converted FDR data have been denied. It has been alleged by the NTSB that converting other FDR information would qualify as the creation of a new agency record, which is not required of an agency under the FOIA. Portions of such converted binary FDR data would reveal details of the final flights by the September 11 aircraft before September 11, 2001, which could be compared to related information already recorded by other federal agencies such as the U.S. BTS.

Such FDR data would presumably corroborate the authenticity of the FDR data itself (which in fact can be shown as suspect), by revealing the operational time and date histories of each aircraft just prior to September 11, 2001 for comparison to purported BTS data.

The binary FDR data file provided by the NTSB can only be utilized by a "Readout and Playback Software" (RAPS) program created by *Flightscape incorporated*. This computer program utilizes algorithms and equations in order to convert the downloaded data from the recorder's binary format into tabular data that will then represent information for various flight parameters.

19

National Transportation Safety Board

Washington, D.C. 20594

Office of the Managing Director

May 27, 2008

Mr. Aidan Monaghan
███████████████████████
██████████
Las Vegas, Nevada 89117

RE: Freedom of Information Act (FOIA) Appeal, Request No. 20080059A

Dear Mr. Monaghan:

I write in response to your letter dated May 15, 2008, in which you appealed the response of the National Transportation Safety Board's FOIA Officer to your FOIA request for "copies of documentation ... which reveal specific data contained within the Solid State Flight Data Recorders (SSFDR's) recovered from ... American Airlines flight 77 and United Airlines flight 93." The Safety Board's FOIA Officer responded to your request on May 9, 2008, and provided all FDR records that the Safety Board has with regard to American Airlines flight 77 and United Airlines flight 93.

Your appeal asserts that the Safety Board is obligated to convert numerous hours of raw FDR data, which the Safety Board provided to you in its response to your request, into tabular files and plots. Your appeal cites 5 U.S.C. § 552(a)(3)(B), which states that agencies should provide requested records "in any form or format requested by the person if the record is readily reproducible by the agency in that form or format." I have determined that the Safety Board must deny your appeal, to the extent that you seek tabular files and plots that include dates and times within the FDR recordings for flights 77 and 93. Providing you with these files would require the Safety Board to create new records in response to your request. In addition, as explained below, to the extent that you seek these records pursuant to § 552(a)(3)(B), please note that these records are not readily reproducible in the format in which you seek them.

First, please note that the FOIA does not require agencies to create records in response to a request or query. See, e.g., Krohn v. Dep't of Justice, 628 F.2d 195, 197-98 (D.C. Cir. 1980); Sakamoto v. EPA, 443 F. Supp. 2d 1182, 1189 (N.D. Cal. 2006); Hudgins v. IRS, 620 F. Supp. 19, 21 (D.D.C. 1985). Furthermore, courts have also held that FOIA requesters may not utilize the FOIA has a means of forcing an agency to complete certain work. See Niagara Mohawk Power Corp. v. U.S. Dep't of Energy, No. 95-0952, transcript at 10 (D.D.C. Feb. 23, 1996) (bench order), vacated & remanded on other grounds, 169 F.3d 16 (D.C. Cir. 1999). If you seek tabular data and plots containing various parameters from the hours of the FDR recordings that precede the accident flights, you must import the raw data that the Safety Board has given you into a tabular data file using specialized software. For your reference, the Safety Board has previously used a software program entitled "Readout and Playback Software (RAPS)," from Flightscape, Inc. This program uses algorithms and equations to convert the data from the recorder's binary format to the text format files that you received in Excel spreadsheets.

National Transportation Safety Board Correspondence (2008)

2

Flightscape offers such FDR software programs commercially, under a licensing agreement; under the Safety Board's own licensing agreement with Flightscape, we are not at liberty to distribute a copy of our software to you. You may contact Flightscape at:

Flightscape, Inc.
36 Antares Drive
Suite 850
Ottawa, Ontario, Canada
K2E 7W5
Tel: +011 (613) 225-0070
http://www.flightscape.com/

In addition, while the FOIA does require that agencies "provide the [requested] record in any form or format requested by the person if the record is readily reproducible in that form or format," 5 U.S.C. § 552(a)(3)(B), courts have held that this provision does not require agencies to engage in extraordinary efforts or procure costly resources in order to reproduce a record in a specific format. Landmark Legal Found. V. EPA, 272 F. Supp. 2d 59, 63 (D.D.C. 2003) (concluding that the agency had not violated the FOIA's "readily reproducible" provision by failing to retain electronic copies of e-mail records that the agency had retained in paper form only, because "the agency may keep its files in a manner that best suits its needs"); see also Chamberlain v. Dep't of Justice, 957 F. Supp. 292, 296 (D.D.C. 1997) (holding that the agency had complied with the FOIA by offering to make visicorder charts, as well as all other original and releasable material that might be damaged by photocopying, available for review, rather than providing copies of the charts); Martin & Merrell, Inc. v. U.S. Customs Serv., 657 F. Supp. 733, 734 (S.D. Fla. 1986) (stating that the FOIA "in no way contemplates that agencies, in providing information to the public, should invest in the most sophisticated and expensive form of technology"). My staff has corresponded with the Vehicle Recorders Division within the Safety Board's Office of Research and Engineering, and confirmed that converting the existing raw FDR data from the numerous hours that preceded flights 77 and 93 would be extremely time-consuming. In addition, isolating the times and providing the data in tabular files and plots would essentially involve creating a new record, as producing the records in the format that you suggest would require an exercise of a vehicle recorders specialist's expertise and judgment. Overall, I have carefully reviewed your appeal and determined that the FOIA does not require the Safety Board to convert the raw data from these FDR recordings into another format.

Based on the foregoing, I have determined that your appeal must be denied, to the extent that it seeks tabular data files and plots. This response constitutes the final action from the National Transportation Safety Board on your appeal. The Freedom of Information Act, 5 U.S.C. § 552, provides for judicial review of this determination.

Sincerely,

Joseph G. Osterman
Managing Director

II Subsequent U.S. BTS FOIA Records for 9/11 Planes Differ from BTS Online Database

According to a FOIA reply from the U.S. BTS, the last known pre-September 11 flights for three of the four aircraft involved in the terrorist attacks of September 11 took place during December, 2000, nine months before the attacks. No pre-September 11 final flight information was provided for AA 77 (N644AA).[1] Why couldn't the BTS account for the last nine months of flight history for these aircraft within FOIA records?

However, a searchable online BTS database produces the following search results for three of the four September 11 aircraft on September 10, 2001:

AA 11 departs San Francisco (SFO): AA 09/10/2001 0198 (flight number) N334AA (tail number) BOS (destination) 22:04 (wheels-off time)[2]

UA 175 departs San Francisco (SFO): UA 09/10/2001 0170 (flight number) N612UA (tail number) BOS (destination) 13:44 (wheels-off time)[3]

UA 93 departs San Francisco (SFO): UA 09/10/2001 0078 (flight number) N591UA (tail number) EWR (destination) 23:15 (wheels-off time)[4]

U.S. BTS FOIA officer Robert Monniere, reported via a subsequent e-mail reply to the author that the FOIA records depicting nine months of missing information for the afore mentioned aircraft, were oddly derived from the very same online database as that which publicly reports the same aircraft as being in normal service during the same period. No explanation was provided within any BTS correspondence as to why no pre-September 11 flight activity was located for AA 77 (N644AA).

A prior FOIA request of the BTS for related records generated the following detailed responses from programmers with the BTS:

—Original Message—
From: Robert.Monniere@dot.gov
To: a_monaghan@xxx.xxx
Sent: Tuesday, July 22, 2008 12:13 PM
Subject: RE: FOIA Request

I received the following response from our Office of Airline Information stating that the agency records indicate that:

"There were no flights in 2001 (August 26 to September 11, 2001) with tail numbers N591UA or N644AA."

—Original Message—
From: Bernard.Stankus@dot.gov
To: a_monaghan@xxx.xxx
Sent: Thursday, July 24, 2008 6:40 AM
Subject: RE: Clarification of FOIA Response

Dear Mr. Monaghan:

A BTS programmer conducted a search of the entire on-time data base (the only data base which captures flight information by tail number) for the tail numbers referenced in your request. We sent you the results of the data search. Please be advised that only domestic scheduled passenger flights are reported in this data base. Charter flights and international flights are not reported. Generally, the major airlines utilize their larger aircraft on the longer international flight segments. Also, the air carriers capture the times needed for reporting purposes by on board computers. If these planes and computers were destroyed in the events of 9-11, I am not sure if the airlines had the capability to capture the necessary data.

Bernie Stankus

It is known that commercial airline aircraft are utilized by local and federal agencies for various training and research and development endeavors. Determining if the four September 11 aircraft were utilized for such exercises prior to the September 11 attacks, in any way that may have affected their performance that day, is difficult to impossible at present due to Federal Bureau of Investigation (FBI) classification of relevant airline and Federal Aviation Administration (FAA) records. Was BTS data altered to conceal pre-September 11 activity of the September 11 planes?

Flight history searches for the tail numbers designating the four September 11 aircraft are also made difficult by the fact that BTS online search engine parameters do not support tail number searches. The comparison data referred to in this section was obtained using date and airport origin and destination information for September 11, 2001. Due to the numerous airports throughout the U.S. potentially serviced by the September 11 aircraft, flight history searches more distant in the past from September 11, 2001 become more difficult.

In addition to the research and development flights referred to earlier, another example of the utilization by federal authorities of a commercial airliner is a June 2002 anti-hijack training exercise sponsored by the FBI and the North American Aerospace Defense Command (NORAD) and involving a Delta Airlines 757.

It may eerily similar to September 11th, two hijackings this morning, but the hijackings are not real. They are a joint U.S.—Canadian terrorism exercise run by NORAD called Amalgam Virgo II. Now the two planes, a Delta 757, with actual Delta pilots in the flight deck, will be hijacked by FBI agents as it makes its trip from Salt Lake City to Honolulu. That plane will be diverted in midair to Elmendorf Air Base in Anchorage, Alaska.[5]

The FBI reported during October of 2008 via a FOIA reply, that FBI records for this exercise could not be located.

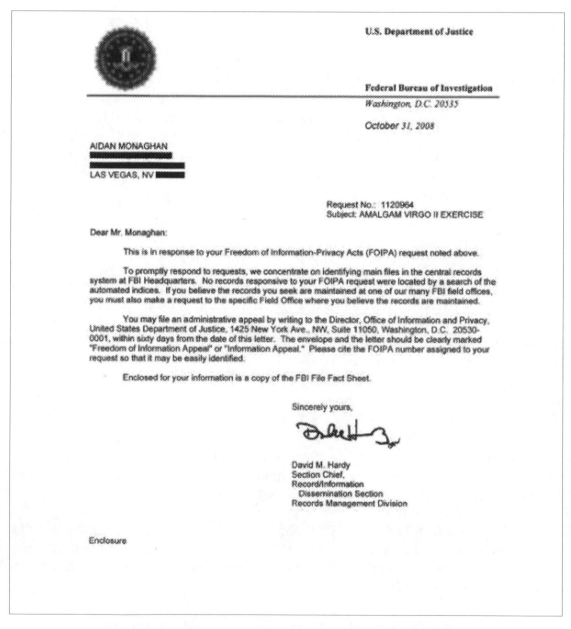

Federal Bureau of Investigation Correspondence (2008)

Other examples of federal agency utilization of commercial aircraft for avionics research and development purposes circa 2001 include the FAA's "Capstone" program. The participating privately owned commercial aircraft contained federally furnished avionics systems.

> The Capstone Program accelerates nationwide efforts to improve aviation safety and efficiency through a multi-year introduction of current and emerging concepts and technologies. Initial validation plans include the installation of government-furnished Global Positioning System (GPS) driven avionics suites in up to 150 commercial aircraft. [6]

One noteworthy example of law enforcement use of a commercial airline aircraft of historic significance and which subsequently became a matter of significant controversy, is the matter of the TWA Boeing 747 aircraft that serviced the airline's July 17, 1996 Flight 800. This flight exploded within minutes after takeoff from New York's John F. Kennedy International Airport.

Subsequent FBI testing of wreckage from TWA 800 revealed the presence of high explosive traces. These findings were not willingly provided to the public and only became known after the information was leaked to news media. Shortly thereafter, federal authorities would conclude that the detected explosive residues could reportedly be attributed to St. Louis, Missouri airport police bomb dog training exercises that occurred just weeks before the TWA 800 catastrophe, utilizing the very same TWA 747 aircraft involved. Interestingly, this very same aircraft was utilized by the U.S. Department of Defense (DoD) as a troop transport during the 1991 Gulf War. However, the registration or tail number for the aircraft used during the St. Louis training exercise was reportedly not recorded.

In fact, between the years 1998 and 2001, NORAD sponsored at least 28 hijack response exercises hosted by U.S. and international commercial airports and utilizing numerous models of commercial aviation aircraft including Boeing 737s and 747s, McDonnell Douglas DC-10s and Lockheed L-1011s.[7] The tail numbers of these aircraft remain unknown. Simulated events that unfolded during these exercises also duplicated those that reportedly unfolded on September 11, 2001 including unrestored losses of aircraft communications following the simulated hijacker takeovers.

Little else is known of these exercises beyond the brief summaries contained within declassified 9/11 Commission records. Attempts to obtain more information via FOIA request have been met with notifications that because NORAD is a bi-national agency of the U.S. and Canada, the organization is not subject to the FOIA.

U.S. Department
of Transportation

1200 New Jersey Avenue, S.E.
Washington, D.C. 20590

**Research and Innovative
Technology Administration**

June 12, 2009

Aidan Monaghan

████████████████
████████████████

Las Vegas, NV ████████████

Re: FOIA Appeal Ref. No. 2009-0024

Dear Mr. Monaghan:

This letter is in response to your April 8, 2009 Freedom of Information Act (FOIA) e-mail submitted to the Bureau of Transportation Statistics (BTS)/Research and Innovative Technology Administration (RITA). In your original request, you asked for copies of records that indicate: the final dates for which departures and/or arrival times are available for the following aircraft registered as of September 11, 2001: American Airlines Flight 11 (N334AA), United Airlines Flight 175 (N612UA), American Airlines Flight 77 (N644AA) and United Airlines Flight 93 N591UA. In your January 16th letter, you indicated that the agency "misunderstood" your request in that you were actually seeking "the final dates for which departure and/or arrival times are available for the said aircraft, regardless of assigned flight number." In response to the agency's March 23, 2009 clarification letter, you submitted the April 8, 2009 e-mail requesting "copies of records indicating the final dates for which departure and/or arrival times are available" for the above aircraft.

Although the agency believes the records which were previously sent in response to your initial request reflect the final departure/arrival dates for the above aircraft, I am enclosing an Excel Spreadsheet which appears responsive to your April 8, 2009 e-mail. I am also sending an electronic copy of the Excel Spreadsheet to your e-mail address. If you have any questions concerning the formats or information, please contact Bernie Stankus @ 202-366-4387. I again want to emphasize that the agency does not have any records that reflect the above aircraft were in commercial air service after September 11, 2001.

Under 49 CFR 7.21, within 30 days from the date you receive this supplemental response, you may file a written appeal. Your appeal should be sent to: The Administrator (RTA-1), RITA, U.S. Department of Transportation, East Building, Room E37-303, 1200 New Jersey Avenue, SE, Washington, DC 20590. Your appeal should include the reference number used above and all information that forms the basis for your appeal. Please mark the envelope, which contains your appeal, with the words: "FOIA Appeal". If you file an appeal, the Administrator's decision will be the final administrative decision.

United States Bureau of Transportation Statistics Correspondence (2009)

Year	Quarter	Month	DayofMonth	DayOfWeek	FlightDate	JniqueCarrie	AirlineID
2000	4	12	30	6	12/30/2000	AA	19805
2000	4	12	31	7	12/31/2000	UA	19977
2000	4	12	31	7	12/31/2000	UA	19977
2000	4	12	30	6	12/30/2000	UA	19977
2000	4	12	30	6	12/30/2000	UA	19977
2000	4	12	30	6	12/30/2000	UA	19977

Carrier	ArrDel15	TailNum	ArrDel30	FlightNum	ArrDelSys15	Origin	ArrDelSys30	OriginCityNam
AA	1	N334AA	0	682	1	SFO	0	San Franci
UA	0	N612UA	0	1742	0	LAX	0	Los Angek
UA	1	N612UA	1	23	1	JFK	1	New York
UA	1	N591UA	1	1238	1	ORD	1	Chicago
UA	0	N591UA	0	951	0	IAD	0	Washingto
UA	0	N591UA	0	642	0	MCI	0	Kansas Cit

III FBI Records Chief Describes Unsuccessful Search for Identifying Records of 9/11 Aircraft Wreckage and FDRs

On August 8, 2008, the Section Chief of the Record/Information Dissemination Section ("RIDS") of the FBI reported to a U.S. district court, the unsuccessful search for records pertaining to the four aircraft identified by the FBI and NTSB as being used during the terrorist attacks of September 11, including two aircraft FDRs. This statement served as a Department of Justice (DoJ) defense exhibit pertaining to the 2008 federal court case Monaghan v. DoJ, for records for the four aircraft used during the September 11 attacks.[8]

SEARCH FOR RECORDS RESPONSIVE TO PLAINTIFF'S REQUEST

Plaintiff's original FOIA request sought "documentation pertaining to any formally and positively identified debris" from the aircraft used in the September 11th attacks. In response to this request, RIDS personnel at FBIHQ understood that any potentially responsive records would have been compiled for law enforcement purposes and would be located in a pending file because of an ongoing law enforcement investigation. RIDS personnel therefore determined that any records would be withheld in their entirety pursuant to 5 U.S.C. § 552(b)(7)(A). The FBI then received a copy of plaintiff's complaint for injunctive relief, later amended, wherein plaintiff requested the FBI to "produce agency records, concerning documentation revealing the process by which wreckage recovered by defendant, from the aircraft used during the terrorist attacks on September 11, 2001, was positively identified by defendant (with the aid of the National Transportation Safety Board) as belonging to the said aircraft, presumably through the use of unique serial number identifying information contained by the said aircraft wreckage, that was collected by defendant and which defendant has improperly withheld from plaintiff." In response to this request, RIDS conducted a search for potentially responsive records at FBIHQ on February 11, 2008. A search of the CRS was conducted using the following subjects: "Airline Debris," "Debris Identification," "Commercial Aircraft," "Aircraft Identification," "Aircraft Debris," "Aircraft Wreckage," "Aircraft," "Recovered Debris," "National Transportation and Safety Bureau," "National Transportation Safety Board," "NTSB," "American Airlines," "American Airlines Flight," "American Airlines Flight Eleven," "American Airlines Flight Number 11," "American Airlines Flight 77," "N334AA," "N612UA," "N644AA," "N591UA," "Flight 175," "Flight 11," "Flight 77," "Flight 93," "Identifying Aircraft Parts," "Factual Report Aviation," "Federal Aviation Administration," "Pentbomb," "Ground Zero," "Freshkills Landfill," and "Fresh Kills Landfill."

Despite this extensive and detailed search effort, RIDS has been unable to locate any FBI records responsive to plaintiffs request. RIDS' search efforts included a verification by the case agent for the investigation. The case agent stated that since the identities of the four hijacked aircraft have never been in question by the FBI, NTSB or FAA (evidence collected after September 11, 2001 has corroborated the fact that American Airlines Flight 11, United Airlines Flight 175, American Airlines Flight 77 and United Flight 93 were the aircraft hijacked), no records would have been generated responsive to plaintiffs request for documents.

IV NTSB: No Records Pertaining to Process of Positive Identification of 9/11 Aircraft Wreckage

Within a July 18, 2008 FOIA response from the NTSB, it is reported that the agency possesses no records indicating how wreckage recovered from the four aircraft used during the terrorist attacks of September 11, was positively identified as belonging to these four planes or even if such wreckage was positively identified at all.[9]

September 11 flight aircraft wreckage, including two FDRs, was reportedly recovered by NTSB personnel, according to NTSB administrators.

Carol Carmody, then Vice-Chairman, of the NTSB, referred to such NTSB wreckage collection activities during public hearings:

> I . . . assured FBI Director Mueller that we would assist in any way we could . . . he called and said, "Could you send us some people to help find the black boxes and help identify aircraft parts.[10]

Marion Blakey, Chairman of the NTSB, is also on public record referring to the NTSB wreckage recovery effort:

> Over 60 Safety Board employees worked around the clock in Virginia, Pennsylvania, New York, and at our headquarters in Washington, D. C., assisting with aircraft parts identification[11]

The afore mentioned aircraft are identified within numerous public NTSB records. Positive wreckage identification was presumably obtained through the use of unique serial number identifying information contained by this wreckage. Within U.S. Code of Federal Regulations (CFR), Title 14, Part 45, it is indicated that all U.S. commercial civil aircraft are required to contain components bearing unique serial number information. Why authorities refuse to release such information that presumably corroborates their accounts is unclear.

V FAA Records Regarding 9/11 Aircraft Unavailable for Release

FOIA requests of the FAA seeking various records regarding the four aircraft involved in the September 11 attacks have been denied by the FAA on the basis that such records are not available for release. These FAA records may now be under the control of the FBI, who have declared that all FBI September 11 information is exempt from disclosure. However, the FAA did not indicate the whereabouts of these records.

FAA failure to release the requested information was not per any established FOIA request exemptions, normally cited by federal agencies that deny FOIA requests.[12]

U.S. Department
of Transportation
**Federal Aviation
Administration**

System Operations Services
800 Independence Avenue, SW.
Washington, DC 20591

DEC 20 2007

Mr. Aidan Monaghan
███████████████████
Las Vegas, NV ███████

Dear Mr. Monaghan:

We are in receipt of your Freedom of Information Act (FOIA 2008-1091, 2008-1244 &
2008-1325) requests received on November 26, December 4, and December 6 seeking records
relating to the events of September 11, 2001. Unfortunately, we are not in a position to release
the said records at this time. When we begin releasing the September 11, 2001, records, we
will respond to all requests in the order in which they were received.

We do apologize in advance for any hardship that this may cause.

Sincerely,

Carol A. Might
Acting Director of System Operations Litigation
Air Traffic Organization

Federal Aviation Administration Correspondence (2007)

VI 9/11 Aircraft 'Black Box' Serial Numbers Mysteriously Absent

Of all major U.S. airline crashes within the U.S. investigated and published by the NTSB during the past 20 plus years, the September 11 'black boxes' are virtually the only ones without published inventory control serial numbers assigned to them.[13]

With FDR serial number information that is virtually always provided within NTSB reports of major U.S. commercial airline crashes that occur within U.S. territory, one can trace an installed device to a particular registered aircraft through manufacturer or airline records.

Because of the criminal nature of the September 11 attacks, the FBI became the lead investigative agency into the September 11 aircraft mishaps, aided by the NTSB upon request.

The following e-mail message was provided to the author by a Susan Stevenson of the NTSB on 12/26/2007, in response to a 12/16/2007 public correspondence e-mail inquiry:

> NTSB investigators rarely encounter a scenario when the identification of an accident aircraft is not apparent. But during those occasions, investigators will record serial numbers of major components, and then contact the manufacturer of those components in an attempt to determine what aircraft the component was installed upon.

Listed here is FDR information provided by the NTSB, for all major U.S. commercial passenger aircraft crashes within U.S. territory, involving major aircraft and/or loss of life, since 1988, including published FDR serial numbers:

Comair Flight 5191, August 27, 2006, CRJ-100, 49 Dead, Fairchild Model F-1000 FDR, Serial Number: 102368 [14]

Chalk's Ocean Airways Flight 101, December 19, 2005, Grumman G-73, 20 Dead (Not equipped with a FDR) [15]

Corporate Airlines Flight 5966, October 19, 2004, HP Jetstream, 13 Dead, Fairchild Model F-1000 FDR, Serial Number: 00511 [16]

Pinnacle Airlines Flight 3701, October 14, 2004, CL-600-2B19, 2 Dead, Fairchild Model F-1000 FDR, Serial Model: 01094 [17]

US Airways Express Flight 5481, January 8, 2003, Beechcraft 1900, 21 Dead, Fairchild Model F-1000 FDR, Serial Number: 01110 [18]

American Airlines Flight 587, November 12, 2001, Airbus 300, 260 Dead, Fairchild Model FA-2100 FDR, Serial Number: 1186 [19]

Alaska Airlines Flight 261, January 31, 2000, Boeing MD-83, 88 Dead, Sundstrand Model FDR, Serial Number: 9182 [20]

American Airlines Flight 1420, June 1, 1999, McDonnell Douglas MD-82, 11 Dead, L3 Model FA-2100 FDR, Serial Number: 00718 [21]

COMAIR Flight 3272, January 9, 1997, Empresa Brasileira de Aeronautica, 29 Dead, Loral Fairchild Model F-1000 FDR, Serial Number: 997 [22]

TWA Flight 800, July 17, 1996, Boeing 747, 230 Dead, Sundstrand Model FDR, Serial Number: 10291 [23]

Valu Jet Flight 592, May 11, 1996, McDonnell Douglas DC-9, 110 Dead, Loral Fairchild Model F-800 FDR, Serial Number: 6132 [24]

Atlantic Southeast Airlines Flight 529, August 21, 1995, EMB-120RT, 8 Dead, Fairchild Digital Model F-800 FDR, Serial Number: 04856 [25]

American Eagle Flight 4184, October 31, 1994, ATR 72, 68 Dead, Loral/Fairchild Model F-800 FDR, Serial Number: 1838 [26]

US Air Flight 427, September 8, 1994, Boeing 737-300, 133 Dead, Loral/Fairchild Data Systems Model F-1000 FDR, Serial Number: 442 [27]

US Air Flight 1016, July 2, 1994, McDonnell Douglas DC-9, 37 Dead, Fairchild S-703 FDR, Serial Number: 00880 [28]

US Air Flight 405, March 22, 1992, Fokker F-28, 27 Dead, Fairchild F-800 FDR, Serial Number: 154 [29]

Atlantic Southeast Airlines Flight 2311, April 5, 1991, Embraer EMB 120, 23 Dead, (Not equipped with a FDR) [30]

United Airlines Flight 585, March 3, 1991, Boeing 737, 25 Dead, Fairchild Model F-800 FDR, Serial Number: 4016 [31]

US Air Flight 1493, February 1, 1991, Boeing 737, 22 Dead, Sundstrand Model FWUS FDR, Serial Number: 692 [32]

United Airlines Flight 232, July 19, 1989, McDonnell Douglas DC 10, 111 Dead, Sundstrand Model 573 FDR, Serial Number: 2159 [33]

> Delta Air Lines Flight 1141, August 31, 1988, Boeing 727, 14 Dead, Lockheed Model 109-D, FDR, Serial Number: 654 [34]

The only other instance of undocumented FDR serial numbers following a major U.S. commercial aircraft crash within U.S. territory during this 20 plus year period seems to be a little known mishap that oddly, occurred on September 11, 1991, exactly 10 years before the September 11 attacks. This report also did not list a FDR manufacturer or model number, possibly because the accident was immediately determined to be the result of negligence on the part of aircraft maintenance personnel.

> Continental Express Flight 2574, September 11, 1991, EMB 120, 14 Dead, FDR Manufacturer, Model & Serial Number Not Available. [35]

VII NTSB Describes Importance of Unpublished September 11 FDR Part Numbers and Serial Numbers

The following is information obtained from the NTSB via online public inquiry requests by the author, regarding FDR part numbers and unique serial numbers required to facilitate the data readouts obtained from the FDRs recovered from AA 77 and UA 93 following the September 11 attacks.

Within a June 5, 2008 response from the NTSB, it is explained why unique FDR serial numbers are required to obtain correct FDR data readouts:

> The exact serial number of the unit delineates manufacturing break points. The serial number is used to identify when a recorder manufacturer switched from a certain memory configuration to another. This information is necessary to perform the correct recovery of the data.[36]

Because the FBI was the lead investigative agency of the attacks of September 11, FAA and airline aircraft records would have presumably been brought under the control of the FBI and made available to the NTSB.

Within a June 11, 2008 inquiry reply from the NTSB, the NTSB implies that when FDR part and serial numbers are not known, they are not published within NTSB reports:

> The Safety Board will include the manufacturer, the part number and the serial number of the recorder in its formal reports (if known).[37]

Because each essential FDR part and serial number was not published, they were presumably not made available to NTSB investigators. And because the contents of each FDR were presumably of great interest to FBI investigators, it is unusual that these FDR part and serial numbers were apparently not utilized in order to best facilitate each data download.

However, because each AA 77 and UA 93 FDR model and manufacturer is known and published within the AA 77 and UA 93 FDR reports, it would seem that the NTSB possibly obtained limited access to information contained within airline aircraft records for AA 77 and UA 93, although FDR model and manufacturer may have been visually evident to a trained observer. Why the NTSB was apparently unable to also obtain or publish the FDR part and serial numbers required to generate proper FDR data readouts is unknown. Presumably, if the recovered AA 77 and UA 93 FDR's did not possess the memory configurations indicated within airline aircraft records, a mismatch could become apparent to NTSB investigators who were simply operating under FBI direction.

According to the NTSB "Flight Data Recorder Handbook for Aviation Accident Investigations", FDR serial numbers are required for data readout:

> Specifically, the following information is required to facilitate data readout: . . . FDR Part number and Serial Number[38]

Additional FDR information was provided by the NTSB within a June 11, 2008 reply, revealing the significance of the apparently unknown part and serial numbers of the FDRs attributed to AA 77 and UA 93:

> Each recorder does have a unique serial number that is assigned by the manufacturer at the time it is made. In addition to the unique serial number there is a part number that associates the unit with a particular family of recorders. Every recorder has a dataplate affixed to the outside of the unit stating the serial number, part number, date of manufacture, TSO certification, power requirements and weight. The part number will stay the same even though subtle changes may be made during the manufacturing lifecycle of the recorder. The manufacturer may change some components within the unit as long as the functionality and interchangeability of the unit remain the same. This is where the serial number becomes important. If a recorder with the same part number comes in we need to know what parts were used to make it and that is tracked by individual serial numbers of the recorder.[39]

VIII September 11 Flight "Black Box" File Time Stamp Precedes FDR Recovery

Following the NTSB recovery of the FDR reportedly from AA 77, its data was subsequently downloaded for examination. The flight data file comprised of the downloaded information was created on Thursday, September 13, 2001 at 11:45pm. However, as reported by USA Today, Pentagon spokesman Army Lt. Col. George Rhynedance announced that the FDR for AA 77 was recovered on Friday, September 14, 2001 at 4am, 4 hours and 15 minutes after the creation of the AA 77 FDR data file, making the alleged file creation time impossible. The AA 77 FDR file was contained within a May 2008 CD release obtained through a FOIA request of the NTSB. [40]

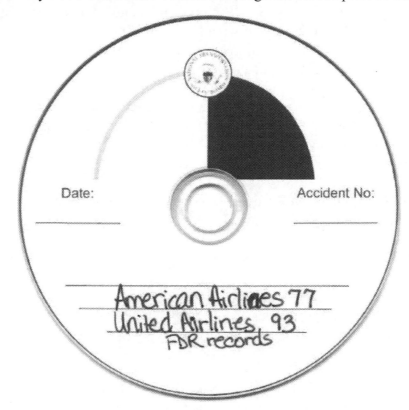

Author's NTSB Copy of AA 77 FDR Data File

IX AFIP: September 11 Hijacker Forensic Identification Records Exempt from Disclosure

The U.S. Armed Forces Institute of Pathology (AFIP) advised via reply to a 2010 FOIA request that evidence collection records confirming the identities of those accused of hijacking the September 11 flights and their presence aboard these flights, are exempt from public disclosure. Although the events of September 11 would seem to be a settled matter for the U.S. federal government, the AFIP attributes this exemption to the September 11 events being subject to a still active federal investigation and also that the release of such records represents an unreasonable invasion of the privacy of relatives of the deceased.

It is interesting to note that passenger victim identifications from the two September 11 airliner crashes in New York City, that were either broadcast live or shortly thereafter, was delegated to local authorities, while passenger victim identifications from the other two September 11 airliner crashes that were not filmed and that were only observed by relatively few if any witnesses, were delegated to the U.S. Department of Defense's AFIP.

DEPARTMENT OF THE ARMY
OFFICE OF THE GENERAL COUNSEL
104 ARMY PENTAGON
WASHINGTON DC 20310-0104

February 4, 2010

Mr. Aidan Monaghan
██████████████████████
Las Vegas, NV ██████████████

Dear Mr. Monaghan:

This letter responds to your Freedom of Information Act (FOIA) appeal dated October 29, 2008. The U.S. Army Medical Command, the Initial Denial Authority (IDA), denied your request to the Armed Forces Institute of Pathology (AFIP) for all records pertaining to the recovery and identification of human remains of those who perished in the September 11, 2001 attacks at the Pentagon and Shanksville, PA.

We apologize for the delay in responding to your appeal. The Army is required to address a large volume of FOIA demands and cannot always respond to appeals as quickly as we would like. We make it our practice to respond to appeals in the order received. The courts have sanctioned this method of handling FOIA cases. *Open America v. Watergate Special Prosecution Force*, 547 F.2d 605, 614-16 (D.C. Cir. 1976).

The IDA withheld the records under Exemptions 6, 7A, and 7C of the FOIA. 5 U.S.C. § 552(b)(6), (b)(7)(A), and (b)(7)(C). After a careful review of the issues presented in your appeal, we have determined that the IDA properly withheld these records. Accordingly, your appeal is denied.

Exemption 6 of the FOIA permits an agency to withhold all information about individuals contained in "personnel and medical files and similar files" if the disclosure of such information would "constitute a clearly unwarranted invasion of personal privacy." 5 U.S.C. § 552(b)(6). Even if a privacy interest in the information is found to exist, the document still may be released if the privacy interest is outweighed by the public interest in disclosure. *See Ripskis v. HUD*, 746 F.2d 1, 3 (D.C. Cir. 1984). The public interest to be considered is "the kind of public interest for which Congress enacted the FOIA," one which "sheds light on an agency's performance of its statutory duties." *Dep't of Justice v. Reporters Comm. for Freedom of the Press*, 489 U.S. 749, 773, 775 (1989).

In order for the information contained in the responsive records to be eligible for protection under Exemption 6, it must first fall within the category of "personnel and medical and similar files." The Supreme Court has interpreted the term "similar files" broadly and has stated that all information which "applies to a particular individual" meets the threshold requirement for Exemption 6 protection. *Dep't of State v. Washington Post*, 456 U.S. 595, 602 (1982). In this case, the referred records withheld

United States Armed Forces Institute of Pathology Correspondence (2010)

3. Secret Service Records Don't Resolve VP Cheney "Bunker" Arrival Time Mystery

The U.S. Secret Service (USSS) provided via reply to a 2010 FOIA request, summaries of USSS White House protectee activity during the September 11 attacks.

Reported in detail are events surrounding White House protectees including Vice President Dick Cheney and USSS efforts to relocate him to the White House Presidential Emergency Operations Center (PEOC) as the attacks unfolded. Cheney's exact PEOC arrival time has since been a matter of some public debate, based in part on 9/11 Commission testimony of then U.S. Department of Transportation (DoT) Secretary Norman Mineta and the recollections of the president's personal secretary and a White House photographer.

Mineta advised the commission during testimony that upon his own arrival at the PEOC, Cheney was already present and directing surveillance of AA 77 as it approached Washington, DC prior to its subsequent reported 9:37am collision with the Pentagon building. Mineta also reported that Cheney's wife is also present at this time. However, official estimates for Cheney's PEOC arrival are just after 9:55am, nearly half an hour after AA 77's official crash time. USSS records presented here, somewhat corroborate the 9/11 Commission's alleged PEOC arrival time for Vice President Cheney. But all official arrival times conflict with the arrival times for the Vice President and Mrs. Cheney provided by Mineta, whose account is corroborated in part by President Bush's personal secretary Ashley Estes and White House photographer David Bohrer. Both Estes and Bohrer witness Vice President Cheney being hurriedly led by Secret Service agents from his White House office to the PEOC shortly after UA 175 impacts WTC 2 at 9:03am.

Much has been made of Cheney's PEOC activity, in light of Secretary Mineta's description of Cheney being incrementally updated by a "young man" of the approach of what Mineta reports as AA 77. Such AA 77 location updates to Cheney reportedly began at a range of 50 miles distant and ended at 10 miles distant.

Also of substantial interest to researchers was a reported question of Cheney by the "young man" within the PEOC as AA 77 was reportedly just 10 miles away: "Do the orders still stand?". A reportedly agitated Cheney answered: "Of course the orders still stand. Have you heard anything to the contrary?". What these alleged orders were or even what exactly unfolded within the PEOC during this time has never been fully explained.

The USSS documents presented here do not contain the identity of the "young man" communicating with the Vice President as reported by Mineta, even though the FOIA request at issue sought information regarding all persons present within the PEOC during the September 11 attacks.

U.S. Department of Homeland Security
UNITED STATES SECRET SERVICE

Aiden Monaghan

APR 2 3 2010

Las Vegas, NV

Re: Freedom of Information Act Appeal - File Numbers 20080330 and 20080331

Dear Mr. Monaghan:

Reference is made to your letter to the United States Secret Service (Secret Service) regarding the above referenced files. Through your letter you appeal the determination of Special Agent in Charge Craig W. Ulmer, Secret Service Freedom of Information and Privacy Acts Officer, that the Secret Service was not maintaining documents responsive to your Freedom of Information Act (FOIA) requests.

Based on your appeal, an additional search was conducted for records responsive to your request, and responsive material was located. This material has now been processed under FOIA and copies of this material are enclosed. However, some information is being withheld from release under the FOIA. No responsive documents have been withheld in their entirety.

The records in question contain information compiled for law enforcement purposes. Pursuant to Title 5, United States Code, sections 552(b)(6) and section 552(b)(7)(C), some information is being withheld since disclosure of this information could reasonably be expected to constitute an unwarranted invasion of privacy. Additional information has also been withheld pursuant to sections (b)(2)(high) and (b)(7)(E) since disclosure of this internal agency information would disclose techniques and procedures for law enforcement investigations, and/or would disclose guidelines for law enforcement investigations or prosecutions if such disclosure could reasonably be expected to risk circumvention of the law.

Finally, please be advised that the Secret Service's search for responsive records yielded information that originated with other federal agencies. This information is being referred to those agencies for direct response to you.

Any denial on appeal is subject to judicial review in the District Court in the district where the complainant resides, has a principal place of business, or in which the agency records are situated, or in the District of Columbia.

Sincerely,

Keith L. Prewitt
Deputy Director

Enclosures

United States Secret Service Correspondence (2010)

DECLASSIFIED BY
b6, b7c
b6, b7c

ON 11/5/08 ~~SECRET~~

Actions of TSD Related to Terrorist Incident (U)
September 12, 2001

(U) 0858 Reported to the EOC for a routine 9:00am PPD Staff Meeting. The first aircraft crash incident was on the EOC monitor.

(U) 0903 – The second aircraft crashed into the World Trade Center. Upon realizing that a terrorist event was underway ADC [b6,b7c] telephoned ADC [b6,b7c] to advise him to notify Branch Chief [b6,b7c] to immediately activate a [b2,b7E] and to report to North Court of the EEOB to move [b2,b7E] assets to [b2,b7E] for response.

(U) 0905 – ADC [b6,b7c] reported to the TSD Duty Desk to instruct the desk (PSS [b6,b7c] to (1) advise all EOD assets to move to [b2,b7E] and respond from that location (2) and page BC [b6,b7c] to call the TSD Duty Desk. [b6,b7c] advises the TSD Duty Desk to page all TSD personnel in the Washington D.C. area to report to their duty station.

(U) 0907 – ADC [b6,b7c] advised BC [b6,b7c] via telephone to activate a [b2,b7E] and to move [b2,b7E] assets to [b2,b7E] [b6,b7c] was advised to alert the DOD Structural collapse team [b2,b7E] at Ft. Belvoir. (Alert will instruct all of the structural collapse personnel associated with the special program that the Secret Service may have a need for their assets and they should report to their duty station.

(U) 0915 – ADC reported to the EOC and was instructed that SAIC Truscott wanted DSAIC [b6,b7c] and [b6,b7c] to report to his office EEOB [b2,b7E] ASAP.

(U) 0918 – ADC [b6,b7c] reported to SAIC Truscott in [b2,b7E]. DSAIC [b6,b7c] and ADC [b6,b7c] discussed briefly with SAIC Truscott the assets that had been deployed to that point. SAIC Truscott was on the phone with one unknown person and [b6,b7c] SAIC Truscott learned that an aircraft had been identified en-route to the Washington area.

(U) 0918 – SAIC Truscott suggested that an relocate to the shelter.

(U) 0926 – EEOB evacuation was initiated by OA Staff and all personnel were departing the building in an orderly but expeditious fashion.

(U) 0926 – ADC [b6,b7c] and SAIC Truscott departed Room 10 en-route to the shelter. DSAIC [b6,b7c] reported to the EOC.

(S) 0930 – ADC [b6,b7c] reported to basement level ZP door and entered. SAIC Truscott and Zotto were already in the area with numerous (10) Presidential and Vice Presidential staff to include Vice President Cheney and NSC Advisor Rice. The Vice President was completing a telephone call at the base of the stairs. Upon completion of the Vice President's call, SAIC Truscott requested that the group proceed to the PEOC.

(U) 0933 – The group entered the PEOC at which time information flow to the Vice President and staff began.

(U) 0941 – CNN reported that a plane had crashed into the Pentagon.

(U) 1130 – ADC [b6,b7c] advised SAIC Truscott that his role as a technical advisor could be better served in the EOC and then reported to the EOC.

(U) 2000 – ADC [b6,b7c] attended a manpower meeting with other PPD staff to discuss staffing for the next 24 hour period.

(U) 2230 – ADC [b6,b7c] reported to the EOC and was briefed by Branch Chief [b6,b7c] and departed for residence.

~~SECRET~~

SECRET

SEPTEMBER 11, 2001

0744 hrs	Angler departed Naval Observatory en route White House.
0757 hrs	Angler arrived White House.
0813 hrs	Author departed Navobs en route Nantucket.
0825 hrs	Author arrived Nantucket.
0857 hrs	Television media reports that a plane crashed into World Trade Center.
0910 hrs	Media reports second plane crashed into other tower at World Trade Center.
0936 hrs	JOC advised the working shift that a plane was heading towards the White House.
0936 hrs	VP shift and supervisor moved Angler to secure location within the White House.
0938 hrs	Plane crashed into Pentagon.
0945 hrs	Author departed Nantucket en route White House.
0945 hrs	Security level Charlie was initiated at Tower.
0952 hrs	Author arrived White House and was moved to secure location.
1020 hrs	Attempt was made to reach SA b6, b7c Bonaire at hotel and cell phone numbers with negative result.
1030 hrs	SA b6, b7c depart en route to Country Day School and Potomac School to pick up Advocate's children.
1030 hrs	SA b6, b7c is pre-positioned at WDC relocation site. Telephone: b6, b7c b6, b7c
1038 hrs	Plane crashed in Pennsylvania.
1045 hrs	Three fighter jets are circling P-56 airspace.
1045 hrs	Per SA b6, b7c, Advocate is en route to her residence.
1045 hrs	SA's b6, b7c are en route to Advocate's residence.

SECRET

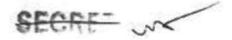

4. Technological Treason? Aviation Automation and the 911 Attacks

The alleged piloting performances of the accused terrorist pilots with no known previous experience behind the controls of a Boeing airliner during the September 11 attacks have surprised more knowledgeable observers. In fact, official evidence presented to demonstrate terrorist pilot control of the said aircraft is either uncorroborated or shown to be anomalous while conversely, there is abundant evidence suggesting an inability of the accused to pilot large Boeing jets. Moreover, the observed and measured flight paths of the September 11 attack aircraft, examined here by the author through observation and calculation, bear characteristics common to the capabilities provided by automated aircraft flight control systems and related commercial aviation technology that emerged just prior to these attacks. The evidence of an unreported use of augmented GPS guided aircraft autopilot systems being responsible for the September 11 aircraft attacks is considered here.

I Availability of GPS Service

U.S. federal government and civil aviation industry publications describe the development and use pre-September 11, 2001, of state-of-the-art systems capable of supporting precise automated navigation of the Boeing 757 and 767 aircraft used that day to a given destination. The Global Positioning System (GPS) is a space-based radio-navigation system that generates accurate positioning, navigation and timing information for civil use at no cost. The information signal can be obtained through the use of GPS signal receiving equipment or aircraft avionics.[1]

Augmented GPS signal service intended to replace dated and expensive U.S. ground-based aviation navigation signals was developed during the mid-to-late 1990s by the FAA and the Raytheon corporation. Serving on Raytheon's Special Advisory Board was "Project for the New American Century" signatory Richard Armitage, although it is unknown precisely when he served in this capacity.[2]

Known as the Wide Area Augmentation System (WAAS), precisely surveyed ground-based Wide-area Reference Stations monitor and collect GPS satellite position signal errors. Ground-based Wide-area Master Stations then transmit corrected GPS position signal information to ground-based Ground Uplink Stations that then transmit the corrected GPS position signal information to orbiting Geostationary Satellites. These satellites then broadcast the corrected positional information back to Earth for use within a GPS-like signal.[3]

Since 1978 through today, dozens of GPS satellites have been launched in what are known as blocks, while some have been occasionally decommissioned.

On May 1, 2000, just 16 months prior September 11, 2001, President Bill Clinton announced that intentionally embedded position and timing errors within GPS data (called Selective Availability or SA) would end. SA was implemented in order to deter abuse of GPS in the national security interest.

> Today, I am pleased to announce that the United States will stop the intentional degradation of the Global Positioning System (GPS) signals available to the public beginning at midnight tonight. We call this degradation feature Selective Availability (SA). This will mean that civilian users of GPS will be able to pinpoint locations up to ten times more accurately than they do now . . . My decision to discontinue SA was based upon a recommendation by the Secretary of Defense in coordination with the Departments of State, Transportation, Commerce, the Director of Central Intelligence, and other Executive Branch Departments and Agencies.[4]

The FAA later announced on August 24, 2000, just 13 months prior to the September 11, 2001 attacks, that the WAAS signal was available for non-public safety related civil use pending final approval by the FAA, which later occurred in 2003. Horizontal and vertical GPS positional data accurate to between one to three meters and sufficient for Category I precision aircraft runway approaches, was now available throughout the contiguous United States.[5][6] Unaugmented GPS service only provided placement accuracy to within 100 meters. Conventional en route aviation navigation beacon signals were only able to provide placement information accurate to within one mile.[7] In fact, Raytheon's then director of satellite navigation systems reported that rescue personnel utilized the newly activated WAAS signal, in order to precisely survey the Ground Zero site following the September 11 attacks.[8]

II Performance Based Navigation

The activation of the WAAS signal contributed significantly to the accuracy of an aircraft navigation and landing procedure system developed during the 1990s known as "Required Navigation Performance" (RNP), which utilizes precisely constructed "highways in the sky" that can be navigated entirely by the autopilot systems of aircraft like those involved in the terrorist attacks of September 11. WAAS enabled RNP technology "pinpoints the location of a fast-moving jet to within yards".[9] Such routes "never vary more than 18 meters—half the wingspan of a Boeing 737".[10] Upon the introduction of the WAAS signal utilized by the RNP system and relying on appropriate aircraft avionics, it was predicted that "a pilot will be able to determine the airplane's vertical and horizontal position within six or seven meters (about 20 to 23 feet)".[11] By another estimate, the WAAS signal provides horizontal and vertical positional accuracy of 1-3 meters, whereas the Instrument Landing System (ILS) antenna arrays that provide precise aircraft centerline placement over the 150-200 foot wide runways of major U.S. airports are accurate to only 7.6 meters in both planes at the middle marker. [12]

RNP "highway in the sky" routes provide for a containment accuracy of 95% within a virtual corridor. Such corridor dimensions are described in terms of nautical miles. In 2003, Raytheon reported that WAAS enabled corridors were as narrow as 243 feet (RNP 0.02). It is noteworthy that the WTC towers were each a comparable 208 feet wide.

> WAAS also supports required navigation performance (RNP) operations, says Raytheon, providing a precision navigation capability down to RNP 0.02 (an accuracy of 0.02nm).[13]

Conversion calculations proceed as follows: 1 nautical mile = 6,076 feet; RNP 0.02 = RNP (0.02 nautical mile radius) x 2 = RNP (121.5 foot radius) x 2 = a 243 foot wide corridor.

According to a Boeing study:

> Accuracy and integrity are expressed in terms of nautical miles and represent a containment radius of a circle centered around the computed FMC position where there is a defined containment probability level of the actual aircraft being inside the containment radius. For accuracy the containment probability level is 95%.[14]

Aviation and popular publications describe a complex 2006 autopilot controlled RNP test flight performed by a Boeing 757 containing Flight Management Systems (FMS) and augmented GPS signal receivers scheduled to be contained by American Airlines and United Airlines 757 and 767 aircraft during the late 1990s, utilizing waypoint coordinate information contained within the aircraft's Flight Management Computer (FMC), that included a descent from a 38,000 foot altitude.

> Guided entirely by autopilot, an Air China Boeing 757 jet last month snaked along a narrow river valley between towering Himalayan peaks . . . the airplane automatically followed the twists of the valley, descending on a precisely plotted highway in the sky toward a runway still out of sight . . . Using global-positioning satellites and on-board instruments, Naverus' navigation technology pinpoints the location of a fast-moving jet to within yards . . ." "You're watching the whole thing unfold. The airplane is turning, going where it's supposed to go . . . it's all automatic."[15]

> For this RNP approach in Tibet, an Air China Boeing 757 was relying on dual GPS receivers, flight path computers and inertial reference systems . . . the aircraft we are on is equipped with Honeywell Pegasus flight management systems and Rockwell Collins multi-mode receivers.[16]

In fact, by 1999, Boeing 757 and 767 aircraft like those involved in the terrorist attacks of September 11 contained digital flight control systems that can "automatically fly the airplanes on pre-selected routes, headings, speed or altitude maneuvers."[17] In fact commercial aviation automation has made it possible for pilots to fly an aircraft as little as three minutes per flight.[18]

III Waypoint Substitution

For U.S. aviation purposes utilizing GPS navigation, a waypoint is a three dimensional location within the National Air Space (NAS), comprised of longitude, latitude and altitude coordinates.[19] RNP supported flight paths and runway approach procedures are comprised of a series of waypoints.[20] The WTC towers themselves occupied waypoint coordinates.[21] FMS facilitated instrument approach procedures involve the interception of waypoint coordinates.[22] By substitution of WTC tower and Pentagon building waypoint coordinates for flight leg terminating waypoint coordinates, a RNP-like waypoint intercept procedure under autopilot control performed by three of the four aircraft destroyed on September 11, 2001, could apparently accomplish the aircraft attacks that were observed.

IV Common Performance Characteristics

A feature supported by RNP approach procedures and utilizing the WAAS signal activated one year before September 11, 2001, is the use of descending constant radius turns, known as Radius-to-Fix (RF) turns.[23] Such turns are similar to the 6 and 330 degree descending turns performed by UA 175 and AA 77 upon their final approaches-to-impact with WTC 2 and the Pentagon building.[24] The point at which AA 77's 330 degree descending right turn terminated would be comparable to the transition to a Final Approach Fix (FAF), from where a straight final runway approach segment would commence.

The Department of Aeronautics and Astronautics at Stanford University described experimental RF turns, similar to those performed by UA 175 and AA 77, following 1998 test flights involving a WAAS prototype:

> The Wide Area Augmentation System (WAAS) . . . allows pilots to fly . . . approaches that cannot necessarily be flown with current instrumentation . . . Complex curved approaches, including approaches turning to a short (less than one mile) final . . . Pathways were constructed from . . . climbing, or descending constant radius arcs . . . Autopilots could use WAAS position and velocity to fly curved trajectories.[25]

The attack aircraft flight paths observed during the September 11 attacks would apparently be reproducible by RNP-like segments used in combination, performed by specialized aircraft avionics systems available and certified prior to September 11, 2001 for use within the Boeing 757 and 767 aircraft used during the attacks. Although WAAS supported flight procedures were not formally supported within the U.S. for public safety critical operations until 2003, it appears that compatible avionics existed within the types of aircraft used during the September 11 attacks circa 2001.

V Necessary Avionics Systems

On September 6, 1996 Rockwell-Collins Commercial Avionics announced plans by Boeing and major commercial airlines, to install Rockwell-Collins Multi-Mode Receiver (MMR) landing systems within their Boeing 757 and 767 aircraft fleets.[26] The MMR system can utilize the WAAS signal as well as the basic GPS signal, the VHF, UHF, VOR navigation signals and eventually the Local Area Augmentation System (LAAS) navigation signal.[27]

On September 7, 1998 Honeywell International announced plans by American Airlines and United Airlines, to install the RNP-capable Pegasus FMS within their Boeing 757 and 767 aircraft fleets, which provide a 150 waypoint route capacity.[28][29]

Operators of 757s and 767s may also choose to upgrade to the recently certified Future Air Navigation System (FANS) FMC (Pegasus), which is Y2K-ready and available. Service bulletins for the 757 and 767 FANS retrofit will be issued upon operator request.[30]

VI Achieved Systems Accuracy

During numerous FAA, U.S. Air Force and National Aeronautics and Space Administration (NASA) sponsored runway approach and touchdown test flights between 1994 and 2002, involving augmented GPS positional signals and the autopilot systems of Boeing 757, 767 and other Boeing 700 series aircraft, horizontal and vertical positional accuracies of just several meters or less were routinely achieved. The four aircraft used to carry out the September 11 terrorist attacks were also Boeing 757-200 and 767-200 model aircraft.

Runways of major U.S. airports like JFK International, Chicago-O'Hare International and Los Angeles International are between 150 and 200 feet wide.[31][32][33] The WTC towers were interestingly each 208 feet wide.[34]

During October of 1994 at NASA's Crows Landing Flight Facility in California, 110 autopilot approaches and touchdowns of a United Airlines Boeing 737 aircraft facilitated by augmented GPS positional signals, were successfully conducted, with "accuracies on the order of a few centimeters" being consistently achieved.[35]

Also during October of 1994, augmented GPS signal flight tests sponsored by the FAA in cooperation with Ohio University were conducted. 50 autopilot approaches and touchdowns were successfully performed by a donated United Parcel Service (UPS) Boeing 757-200 series aircraft. The augmented GPS positional signal was integrated into the aircraft FMS.[36]

During July and August of 1995, Honeywell, Boeing and NASA sponsored tests using NASA's Boeing 757-200 test aircraft and performed 75 autopilot approaches and touchdowns.

The predicted augmented GPS system aircraft positional accuracy of 1-2 meters was successfully achieved.[37][38]

During October and December of 1998, WAAS supported enroute navigation and Category I instrument aircraft runway approaches were performed over the northern Atlantic ocean and in the nation of Chile, using the FAA's 727 test aircraft. Overall aircraft positional accuracies of 3-4 meters were successfully achieved.[39][40]

During August of 1999, multiple augmented GPS signal guided autopilot approach and touchdown tests were performed using a donated UPS 767 aircraft. These tests were sponsored by the FAA and were centered on the prototype GPS-based LAAS system, which is intended to compliment the FAA's WAAS service. The LAAS signal can provide aircraft positional accuracy of less than one meter horizontally and vertically.[41]

On August 25, 2001, a Fed-Ex 727-200 aircraft equipped with a Rockwell-Collins GNLU-930 Multi-Mode Receiver, conducted six full autopilot approaches and touchdowns during joint U.S. Air Force and Raytheon sponsored test flights, using the Joint Precision Approach and Landing System (JPALS), the military augmented GPS counterpart of the civil LAAS system.[42]

On January 17, 2002, a series of autopilot approaches, touchdowns and rollouts, were conducted to further test the LAAS system with a Fed-Ex Boeing 737-900, equipped with a Rockwell-Collins GLU-920 Multi-Mode receiver. The augmented GPS capable GLU-920 Multi-Mode receiver pre-dates September, 2001 and is designed for use within the Boeing 757-200 and 767-200 model aircraft, like those used during the September 11 attacks.[43][44][45]

VII Automatic Flight Control Override Concept

On October 9, 2001, Cubic Defense Systems, Inc. applied for a U.S. patent for a system that removes control of an aircraft from its pilot and utilizes an aircraft's autopilot system to implement an uninterruptable programmed autopilot flight plan in order to navigate an aircraft to a desired destination during an emergency. This would be accomplished through the use of electronic or mechanical relays that become activated by pilot operation of an aircraft hijack notification system. Surprisingly to some, none of the four aircraft destroyed on September 11, 2001 are known to have entered unique transponder hijack notification codes.

One optional feature of the Cubic system is termination of an aircraft's ability to communicate. In two cases, alleged hijacker communications reportedly aimed at passengers on-board AA 11 and United Airlines flight 93 (UA 93) on September 11, 2001 were heard instead by air traffic controllers. In fact, it is conceded by the FAA that these broadcast's origins are unknown.

The Cubic patent also references Honeywell's 1995 augmented GPS flight navigation research and development, apparently as a signal navigation aid. The system also envisions the use of new aircraft flight instructions transmitted by a remote sender, that would override aircraft functions already underway and direct an aircraft autopilot system to navigate an aircraft to a predetermined destination.[46] A data link interface between an aircraft FMS and the Management Unit for the Aircraft Communication Addressing and Reporting System (ACARS), was developed during the early 1990s. This communication system allows for a flight plan update within an aircraft FMS in mid-flight.[47] An aircraft autopilot system is part of the FMS.

VIII Autopilot Override of Pilot Control

The development of the capability of an aircraft FMC to direct an automatic takeover of aircraft control away from a pilot and turn over control to its autopilot system including Boeing 757's, was underway circa September 11, 2001. The development of a collision avoidance, control override capability utilizing a Boeing 757 is documented as early as 1999. Boeing 757s and 767s containing common avionics, were used during the September 11 attacks.

> Ultimately, if required, the system could initiate an automatically flown evasive maneuver. Validation flights were completed at the NASA Wallops Flight Facility and in-flight demonstrations of the system were completed at Minneapolis-St. Paul International Airport in November 1999 for FAA officials and other Government and industry representatives. The NASA B-757 ARIES and a Honeywell Gulfstream IV (G-IV) were used in the flight test effort.[48]

In 2003, "Aviation Week" and Honeywell described the continued development of "ground proximity warning systems" that can allow a GPS-guided aircraft autopilot system to take away control of an aircraft from a pilot during emergencies. Honeywell state-of-the-art FMSs were used by the four aircraft involved in the September 11 attacks.

> Assisted recovery builds on existing enhanced ground proximity warning systems (EGPWS), autopilot or fly-by-wire technologies to prevent an aircraft from crashing into terrain or buildings . . . If pilots don't respond to warnings within a certain amount of time, assisted recovery directs autopilot or fly-by-wire control systems to steer aircraft away from a crash.[49]

A 2005 report on ground proximity warning systems stated that the Boeing 767s that were crashed into the WTC on September 11, 2001 relied on navigation databases that contained the exact locations of the WTC towers:

> The hijacked passenger jets that hit the World Trade Center buildings were equipped with EGPWS . . . The twin towers were in the database[50]

IX Remote Flight Plan Transmission

The capability to remotely transmit altered aircraft flight plan data via remote data link transmissions, directly into Boeing 757 and 767 aircraft FMCs for use by aircraft autopilot systems was technologically available circa 2001.

Developed in 1999 and technologically supported by the FANS-capable (Future Air Navigation System) Honeywell Pegasus FMS for Boeing 757s and 767s by year 2000, Dynamic Airborne Reroute Procedure (DARP) technology enables aircraft course changes via modified flight plan waypoints, remotely transmitted and installed into aircraft FMCs by VHF or SATCOM (satellite communications) transmission uplinks.

> Dynamic Rerouting, meaning the ability of controllers . . . to change a filed routing once the flight is in progress . . ." The new flight plan with all new waypoints goes into the data link to the comm satellite and is then downlinked into the FMSes of the individual aircraft," . . . "And 'Wow,' say all the old pilots, 'Untouched by human hands!'" . . . Our [dispatch] computer uplinks a route into the FMS that is identified as 'Route 2.' [You're already flying 'Route 1.'] [51]

A January, 2002 description of the capabilities of the Pegasus FMS for Boeing 757s and 767s continues:

> AOC (airline operations center) data link is an optional feature of the Pegasus FMC. This feature provides data link communication of . . . route modifications . . . directly into the FMC (flight management computer).[52]

A May, 2000, Boeing explanation of the capabilities of the Pegasus FMS for Boeing 757s and 767s elaborates:

> A route request may either be a route modified by the crew, or a route which has been sent to the airplane from the Airline Data System.[53]

> The route can be sent by airline operations directly to the ATC Facility via AIDC, for example, for review and uplink to the aircraft.[54]

Like WAAS, DARP capable avionics were present circa 2001 but procedures for its official use were apparently pending:

> At the time of the airworthiness approval of the 757/767 (Pegasus '00) FANS 1 FMC, the operational requirements . . . for providing . . . Dynamic Airborne Route Planning (DARP) based on FANS 1 communication capability were not determined.[55]

By June, 2001, DARP technology was reportedly available but not fully operational:

> Dynamic rerouting (DARP) is not fully operational—Technology is available.[56]

The May, 2000, data-link descriptions for the Pegasus FMS for Boeing 757s and 767s continue:

> Three independent VHF systems (radios and antennas) are installed on the airplane to provide line of sight voice and data communication.[57]

> Satellite communications (SATCOM) may be provided for remote communications where terrestrial contact is unavailable, or by airline policy regardless of the state of other communication capabilities.[58]

> The FMC has the capability to store two routes, designated as route 1 and route 2. The route which defines the flight plan along which the airplane is to be flown is the active route.[59]

A FAA publication description of DARP capability to remotely modify active flight plans already being executed by certain aircraft FMSs reported:

> Planned Airborne Re-route Procedure—DARP (Data link Aircraft): AOC (airline operations center) will plan the re-route and uplink the route to the aircraft, commencing from the waypoint on the current route, ahead of the Aircraft and finishing at destination. Note: Some Flight Management Systems allow AOC uplinks to the Active Route. It is recommended that all AOC route uplinks are directed to the Inactive Route.[60]

X Superior GPS Service During Attacks

Following the deactivation of Selective Availability (SA), measured GPS positioning quality is most affected by GPS satellite geometric strength, represented by a numerical measure known as Geometric Dilution of Precision (GDOP).

Or in other words, more GPS satellites spread throughout the sky, provide better placement information to the user than those that might be concentrated in just one portion of the sky.

> Geometric Dilution of Precision (GDOP) is a GPS term used in geomatics engineering to describe the geometric strength of satellite configuration on GPS accuracy . . . the greater the number of satellites, the better the value of GDOP.[61]

During the impact of UA 175, the maximum number of eleven GPS/WAAS satellites for the entire daylight period were visible from the latitude/longitude coordinates of the WTC (40° 42' 42" N, 74° 0' 45" W).

Visibility

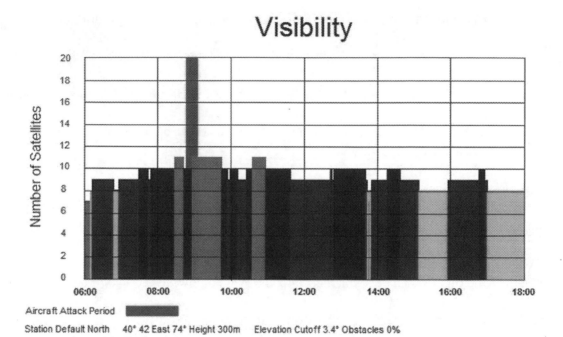

Aircraft Attack Period

Station Default North   40° 42 East 74° Height 300m   Elevation Cutoff 3.4° Obstacles 0%
Time 9/11/2001 06:00 - 9/11/2001 18:00 Satellites 36 GPS 27 WAAS 9

Rendering of GPS Satellite Visibility from WTC Coordinates on September 11, 2001

Visibility

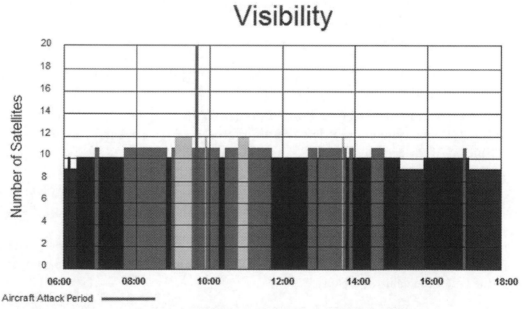

Aircraft Attack Period

Station Default North 38° 52' East 77° 3' Height 300m   Elevation Cutoff 10° Obstacles 0%
Time 9/11/2001 06:00 - 9/11/2001 18:00 Satellites 36 GPS 27 WAAS 9

Rendering of GPS Satellite Visibility from Pentagon Coordinates on September 11, 2001

The impact of AA 11 with WTC 1 occurred while ten of eleven GPS/WAAS satellites were visible, just five minutes after the expiration of the first of two short periods of maximum GPS/WAAS satellite visibility from the WTC coordinates. The period of eleven visible GPS/WAAS satellites from the coordinates of the WTC occupied only 12% of the hours between sunrise and sunset on September 11, 2001. It was during this brief period of virtually maximum GPS/WAAS satellite visibility from the WTC that the aircraft attacks at the WTC unfolded. Similarly superior GPS service also existed from the coordinates of the Pentagon building in Arlington, VA during the reported impact of AA 77. This impact occurred less than ten minutes after the expiration of the longest period of the maximum twelve GPS/WAAS satellites visible from the Pentagon coordinates.

During the aircraft impact period at the WTC, Geometric Dilution of Precision (GDOP) was valued at approximately 2 to 2.3. The maximum GDOP value during the hours between sunrise and sunset on September 11, 2001 was approximately 1.5.

GDOP values of note are as follows:

> 1-2 Excellent: At this confidence level, positional measurements are considered accurate enough to meet all but the most sensitive applications; 2-5 Good: Represents a level that marks the minimum appropriate for making business decisions. Positional measurements could be used to make reliable in-route navigation suggestions to the user.[62]

These GPS findings were obtained utilizing the Trimble GPS planning software, which utilized the GPS almanac file generated by the GPS satellite constellation on September 11, 2001 and is currently hosted by the website of the U.S. Coast Guard.[63][64]

XI Unreliable Official Evidence

Because the FDRs for AA 11 and UA 175 were not recovered, details regarding the modes of operation of each aircraft are not known. Therefore, the official allegation that these flights were actually piloted by those accused, is at best difficult to prove.

The FDRs for AA 77 and UA 93 were recovered and indicate human pilot control of each aircraft. However, the FDR readout file for AA 77 was completed four hours and fifteen minutes before the said FDR was actually recovered, suggesting potentially false or altered FDR information.[65] And the FDRs for AA 77 and UA 93 are virtually the only ones during the previous 20 years of major NTSB U.S. aviation mishap investigations, for which unique inventory control serial numbers were not published.[66] Such serial numbers are required to facilitate FDR data readouts.[67] In fact, the NTSB possesses no records pertaining to the positive identification of the FDRs for AA 77 and UA 93.[68]

XII Accused Hijackers Reportedly Incapable Avionics Operators

Apparently suspect information obtained from the afore mentioned FDRs for AA 77 and UA 93, indicates the performance of numerous and complex autopilot mode changes by the accused hijack pilots of each attack aircraft.[69] However, declassified records generated by the 9/11 Commission contain interviews of United Airlines personnel expert at operating the flight control systems of Boeing 757s and 767s, who describe the likely inability of the said hijackers to perform the flight control operations alleged:

> Entering changes to the auto pilot is something that terrorist pilots probably would not have been trained or able to do. Even the United senior pilot, who instructs on how to do that, said that he always has to pause before he makes such corrections to make sure he remembered how to enter the change.[70]

By the time of their reported takeovers by accused hijackers, each September 11 flight was likely operating in autopilot mode. Therefore, the alleged manual hijacker control of each flight required a disengagement of autopilot operation via controls located upon the Mode Control Panel (MCP). Moreover, it has also been speculated that the alleged hijackers guided their aircraft substantial distances to their targets by entering airport codes into the Multifunction Control and Display Unit (MCDU), for those airports nearest the WTC and the Pentagon. A pilot interfaces with an aircraft FMS via the MCDU keypad. As noted by the afore mentioned United Airlines senior pilot, such autopilot mode changes would have likely been beyond the ability of amateur hijackers under even normal conditions. Such changes by amateur hijackers seem even less likely under what were reportedly violent hijacking environments aboard each September 11 flight.

XIII Evidence of Precise Navigation

Contributing to the plausibility of covert precision automated control of the two aircraft striking the WTC and the seeming unlikelihood that accused amateurs piloted them, is that each aircraft struck precisely the bottom regions of the only sections within each WTC tower only recently upgraded with what were reportedly thermal protection materials. This would be consistent with and suggest a clandestine relationship between the visually spectacular aircraft attacks upon the WTC and activity pre-September 11, 2001 within each WTC aircraft impact region, intended to cause structural failure not generated by the aircraft attacks themselves, but simply contribute to an appearance of structural failures caused by these aircraft impacts.[71]

Floors 92 and above were re-fireproofed by the Port Authority of NY/NJ between 1995-2000 within WTC 1. WTC 1 was struck at floor 94 by AA 11. Floors 77 and above were re-fireproofed between 1995-2000 within WTC 2. WTC 2 was struck at floor 78 by UA 175.[72][73]

XIV Implications of September 11 Flight Transponder Signal Losses

Since September 11, 2001, it has generally been accepted by the media and later the 9/11 Commission itself, that the loss of Secondary Surveillance Radar (SSR) information for three of the four September 11 flights was caused by accused hijackers who allegedly seized control of the aircraft flight decks and manually turned off each plane's Mode S (Mode Select) transponder, presumably for the purpose of evading detection and interception by U.S. air defense systems. However, this conclusion appears to be based only on circumstantial evidence—the simple loss of SSR flight data to ATC—and seems unsupported by conclusive information. Moreover, ATC was nevertheless still able to label and track September 11 flight primary radar returns and even include groundspeed information.

Perhaps the most significant consequence of lost September 11 flight SSR data to ATC was a circumstantial impression of accused hijacker flight deck takeovers. As can be shown, aircraft Mode S transponder SSR information can be caused to vanish from ATC radar screens by other documented means.

From the FAA:

> The secondary radar uses a second radar antenna attached to the top of the primary radar antenna to transmit and receive area aircraft data for barometric altitude, identification code, and emergency conditions. Military, commercial, and some general aviation aircraft have transponders that automatically respond to a signal from the secondary radar by reporting an identification code and altitude . . . The primary surveillance radar uses a continually rotating antenna mounted on a tower to transmit electromagnetic waves that reflect, or backscatter, from the surface of aircraft up to 60 miles from the radar.[74]

Just prior to year 2000, a major modernization of the FAA's entire Air Route Traffic Control Center computers in the continental United States was scheduled to be completed:

> The computers receive, process, coordinate, distribute, and track information on aircraft movement throughout the nation's airspace that includes oceanic international air traffic. The computers provide data interfaces to all types of FAA facilities . . . and the military.[75]

In the case of UA 175, although its transponder-broadcasted flight ID number reportedly changed several times following its alleged hijacking, the transponder itself continued to broadcast unlike the other three flights, making it known to the Traffic Collision Avoidance Systems (TCAS) of nearby aircraft. TCAS avionics will warn aircraft flight crews and FMSs of mid-air collision risks posed by similarly equipped aircraft.

Of the four wayward September 11 flights, only UA 175 experienced near mid-air collisions with other non-wayward commercial flights. These were Delta Flight 2315, US Airways Flight 542 and Midwest Airlines Flight 7. [76]

Coincidentally or not, UA 175 was also the only September 11 flight with a transponder that continued to operate following its unauthorized course change, helping it avoid at least one mid-air collision with a TCAS equipped flight and in fact facilitating its own impact with WTC 2.

Referring to UA 175 and US Airways Flight 542:

> Shortly after that, the hijacked plane was headed straight for a US Airways flight. The US Airways plane's collision-avoidance system detected the approaching plane and advised the US Airways pilot to descend, which he did, averting a collision.[77]

Delta Flight 2315 and US Airways Flight 542 were TCAS compatible Boeing 737s. Midwest Airlines Flight 7 was a TCAS compatible DC-9. The role played by TCAS during UA 175's conflicts with the Delta and Midwest flights is unclear.

Interestingly, for parties with access the FAA's "Host" ATC computer system provided an ability to anticipate route conflicts like those experienced between UA 175 and Delta 2315, US Airways 542 and Midwest 7, based on filed aircraft flight plans:

> HCS is the key information processing system in FAA's en route environment. It processes radar surveillance data, processes flight plans, links filed flight plans with actual aircraft flight tracks, provides alerts of projected aircraft separation violations (i.e., conflicts). [78]

Coincidentally or not, UA 175's transponder was reportedly unique to at least the United Airlines fleet, but could nevertheless be turned off.

> An Air Traffic Control supervisor at New York Center opined that the transponder on United 175 was a newer model peculiar to the United-operated B767 fleet that could not be turned off. That was the supervisor's possible explanation of why the transponder on United 175 changed code as opposed to being turned off. A senior pilot from both United and American Airlines, familiar with cockpit details, each separately demonstrated how transponders were manipulated in the cockpit and conclusively demonstrated that the transponder in United 175 could have easily been turned off.[79]

The four September 11 flights reportedly contained what are known as Mode S transponders:

> The Mode S transponders aboard Boeing 767 and 757 aircraft, such as those used on 9/11 as "flying bombs," deliver aircraft identification and altitude and can supplement FAA's radar by

"providing ATC and traffic alert collision avoidance system (TCAS)-equipped aircraft the ability to determine position and heading information," according to DoT.[80]

Mode S transponders transmit information about the aircraft to the Secondary Surveillance Radar (SSR) system, TCAS receivers on board aircraft . . . This information includes the call sign of the aircraft and/or the transponder's permanent ICAO 24-bit address in the form of a hex code.[81]

According to a safety bulletin published by the International Civil Aviation Authority (ICAO), a given Mode S transponder broadcast can be suppressed or "jammed" by another Mode S transponder broadcasting via the same unique ICAO 24-bit aircraft address already assigned to the given aircraft, causing the given aircraft's SSR flight information to disappear from ATC radar displays, not unlike the disappearance of SSR information for all but one of the September 11 flights. However, the same circumstances can also cause a given aircraft's transponder to become invisible to the TCAS systems of other aircraft, increasing the risk of mid-air collisions. In this case, only an aircraft operator with access to HCS conflict alert information could evade other non-wayward flights.

When two (or more) aircraft with the same (duplicate) ICAO 24-bit aircraft address are operating within range of a specific Mode S interrogator, then potentially hazardous situations can arise: One (or more) of the aircraft involved may be assessed by the Mode S interrogator to be a false or reflected echo, and subsequently ignored. These aircraft will not then be displayed to air traffic controllers.[82]

To date, only military aircraft seem to be capable of mid-flight changes of the 24-bit aircraft address that is contained within its Mode S transponder broadcasts:

Military use of 24-bit aircraft addresses: The relatively large number of aircraft addresses for military use allows rotating the assignments of 24-bit addresses on military aircraft on a frequent basis. This rotation of 24-bit addresses however must not be done during flight. SSR Mode S Interrogators & Radar trackers. The uniqueness property of the 24-bit aircraft address is important for the unambiguous identification of the aircraft. Effects of duplicate addresses are unpredictable. This can cause synchronous garbling, radar track swapping or dropping.[83]

Despite September 11 flight transponder signal losses, ATC was still able to track these flights, complicating the general assumption that September 11 flight transponders were manually turned off by hijackers to evade detection and interception by U.S. air defenses.

Regarding ATC's surveillance of AA 77:

The radar track is untagged, so he attaches a data box to it with the word "LOOK" in it. This will allow other controllers to quickly spot the aircraft. It also causes its ground speed to appear on the screen.[84]

In fact, all of the September 11 flight transponder operation references within the *9/11 Commission Report* only seem to infer that a loss of SSR ATC data was due to the otherwise unsupported theorized conclusion that September 11 flight transponders were manually deactivated by accused hijackers.

> At 8:54, the aircraft deviated from its assigned course, turning south. Two minutes later the transponder was turned off and even primary radar contact with the aircraft was lost.[85]

> On 9/11, the terrorists turned off the transponders on three of the four hijacked aircraft.[86]

> At 8:21, American 11 turned off its transponder, immediately degrading the information available about the aircraft.[87]

> Because the hijackers had turned off the plane's transponder, NEADS personnel spent the next minutes searching their radar scopes for the primary radar return. American 11 struck the North Tower at 8:46.[88]

> The failure to find a primary radar return for American 77 led us to investigate this issue further. Radar reconstructions performed after 9/11 reveal that FAA radar equipment tracked the flight from the moment its transponder was turned off at 8:56.[89]

> American 11, the transponder signal was turned off at 8:21; on United 175, the code was changed at 8:47; on American 77, the signal was turned off at 8:56; and on United 93, the signal was turned off at 9:41.[90]

A view not considered by September 11 analysts and historians is that alleged hijacker deactivations of aircraft transponders actually jeopardized their reported goals by making their flights invisible to other flights and thus subject to mid-air collisions. Clearly, remote access to and control of September 11 flight automated control systems could be facilitated for parties with access to filed HCS flight plan information for planes within the proximity of these flights. In this case, the jeopardy created by September 11 flight transponder signal losses could be overcome.

Mysteriously, just minutes before its reported crash at just after 10am, UA 93's SSR data once again reportedly became visible to ATC at an altitude of 7,500 feet.[91] Would the reappearance of SSR information to ATC from UA 93 just three minutes before it reportedly nose dived into the ground, be evidence of long range transponder jamming that was interrupted by UA 93's reduced altitude and proximity to south western Pennsylvania's elevated mountainous terrain?

5. Observed and Measured In-Flight Turns Suggests Superior Control of 9/11 WTC Aircraft

Video footage depicts UA 175 impacting WTC 2 on September 11, 2001 in New York City, via a trajectory comprised of two separate banked turns. Trigonometric calculations examined here will reveal that the second turn was apparently not required to generate impact. The first turn, which maintains a remarkably steady angle of bank (AoB), is evident at 1.2 miles before impact.[1] Although human control of UA 175's observed maneuvers cannot be ruled out, the precise coordination of variables such as the selections of a correct bank angle and turn start time for this first turn, apparently pose serious challenges to the unaided human control hypothesis. The observed turn stability favors the use of autopilot operation, either functioning in a conventional course control mode or in Control Wheel Steering (CWS) mode. The probability that either of these two control systems were used is addressed. However, flight deck images of United and American airlines 757s and 767s suggest that such CWS functions may have been disabled circa 2001.

Constant radius turns utilizing plotted waypoints during commercial aviation operations, are routinely supported by augmented GPS navigation service and related commercial FMSs already available circa 2001.[2] As will be seen, the implementation of UA 175's observed 1.2 mile constant radius turn, seconds earlier or later than observed, would apparently result in UA 175 missing WTC 2. Estimates of the likely effect of existing crosswinds upon UA 175's approach to WTC 2 are also considered. It is noted that a projected impact via the first observed banked turn would have occurred under crosswind conditions capable of generating between 122 and 134 approximate total feet of lateral displacement from the calculated final position of the aircraft if not affected by such crosswinds. Therefore, a precise consideration of these crosswinds was seemingly incorporated into the 20 degree banked turn of UA 175, either by fortuitous human estimation or by more reliable vector triangle calculations performed by aircraft FMSs operating in autopilot mode. Aircraft distances and other calculations are based on a reported aircraft speed for UA 175 of 799 feet per second at impact, as well as upon measured times to impact. [3]

The observed speeds of both attack aircraft were extreme by comparison to the typical speeds of similarly descending aircraft during normal operation. While creating significantly less response time for possible human hijacker pilot course corrections during final target approaches that would demand superior control surface operation, a general vector analysis considering the final course and speed for each aircraft suggests that the unusually high speeds observed would generate greater accuracy of the aircraft while enroute to their targets. Greater speeds would result in smaller course deflection angles and ground track displacements, created by existing and potential crosswinds. (See Appendix section for trajectory calculations.)

It can be shown that UA 175's quite stable next-to-final 20 degree banked turn toward WTC 2 alone without correction, would apparently have led to the impact of the plane with the center of the south face of the tower. At approximately 2.5 seconds prior to its impact, UA 175 dramatically banks an additional 18 degrees to its left, apparently generating an estimated lateral movement of just 19 feet closer to the center of the south face of the tower.[4] This approximate measure of 18 degrees of bank is arrived at by subtracting the approximately 20 degree observed bank angle of UA 175 while enroute to WTC 2 during 5.5 of its final eight seconds of flight, from the 38 degree angle of impact.

There appear to be three possible explanations for the observed final 18 degree roll of UA 175 prior to impact with WTC 2:

1.) The roll was the final component of an automated flight plan under augmented GPS-guided autopilot control, not required to cause impact;

2.) The roll was an unusual automated correction of a crosswind induced tracking error of the observed 20 degree mile-long banked turn, via a flight plan under augmented GPS-guided autopilot control;

3.) The roll was an attempt by an accused hijacker pilot to assure an impact with WTC 2.

The third explanation is complicated by the apparent fact that the dramatic final 18 degree roll was not required to generate impact. The second explanation is complicated by the likelihood that a crosswind induced tracking error correction would be performed more subtly or incrementally by an autopilot system. The first and second explanations are also potentially complicated by possible bank angle/rate of turn limits imposed by airline FMS configurations that may restrict 38 degree banks under autopilot control without modification. A possible rationale for a covertly controlled and unnecessary final 18 degree roll under autopilot control, would be to create a visual impression of active human control where there was none.

Adding or subtracting just five degrees of bank angle to or from UA 175's 20 degree banked next-to-final turn from 1.2 miles distant from WTC 2, results in displacements of approximately 100 feet respectively to the left and right of the observed flight path and the aircraft substantially missing the tower's center by a distance of greater than half its wingspan. This would be the case even with respect to a flight path that would cause the plane to impact the tower's center.

In fact, the type of descending constant radius turn observed during UA 175's next-to-final 20 degree banked turn before impact, is specifically described as being supported by augmented GPS service activated one year prior to September 11, 2001 and related Boeing 767 FMSs during its research and development period in 1998:

The Wide Area Augmentation System (WAAS) . . . allows pilots to fly . . . approaches that cannot necessarily be flown with current instrumentation . . . Complex curved approaches, including approaches turning to a short (less than one mile) final . . . Pathways were constructed from . . . climbing, or descending constant radius arcs . . . Autopilots could use WAAS position and velocity to fly curved trajectories.[5]

I Twenty Degree Bank Angle Initiation Time

Using as a reference rate, UA 175's required 2.5 seconds to bank an additional 18 degrees beyond the 20 degree bank angle observed just prior to impact with WTC 2, it is estimated that UA 175 may have required 2.7 seconds to achieve the said bank angle of 20 degrees beyond the initial observed bank angle of 0 degrees, while still out of view behind the tower. Therefore, UA 175 may have started its 20 degree precisely banked turn toward WTC 2 from a distance of at least 1.6 miles, only 1.2 miles of which was observed.

II UA 175's Turn Timing

Based on observations, it is known that UA 175 was traveling an apparently wings-level and descending trajectory at a rate of possibly greater than the recorded 799f/s at impact due to its angle of descent, before beginning its observed next-to-final 20 degree banked turn toward WTC 2. The official ground speed estimate for UA 175 referred to here was based on a NIST study of video frames of UA 175 only fractions of a second from impact with WTC 2 and while it was in nearly level flight.

To have begun this turn toward the tower just fractions of a second sooner or later than observed, would necessarily result in a shift of the observed turn arc short of or beyond the tower, at a shift rate of at least 799f/s and result in UA 175 missing the 208 foot wide WTC 2.

Interception of a target via a constant radius turn requires a precise coordination of two variables:

1.) The selection of a turn with the correct bank angle.

2.) The selection of the correct start time for the turn with the correct bank angle.

Once again, the observed mile long-plus, 20 degree banked turn of UA 175, would apparently have generated impact with WTC 2 without the final 18 degree roll.

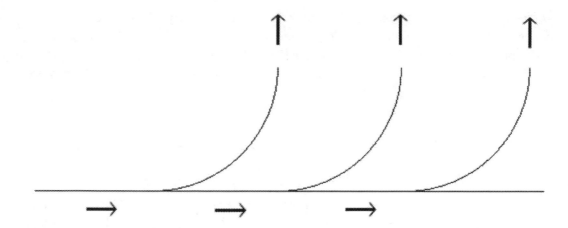

Identical Turn Arcs Originating from and Arriving at Different Locations

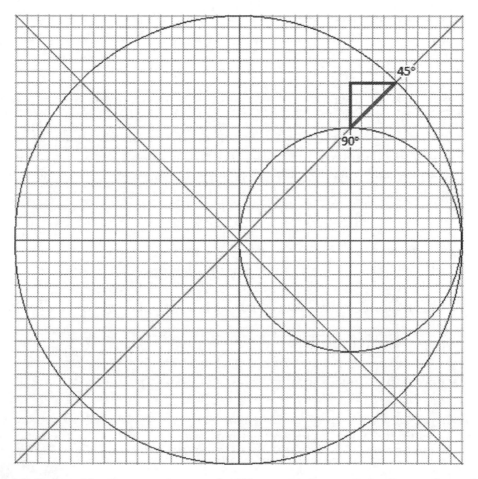

Graphed Relationship Between Turns of Different Radiuses; Turn Separation Distance
Determined by Pythagorean's Theorem

The said 20 degree banked turn also seems to contain no other corrective movements. It is noteworthy that UA 175's projected successful impact with WTC 2, while maintaining its original 20 degree banked turn, would have occurred under crosswind conditions capable of generating between 122 and 134 feet of lateral drift during the aircraft's eight second observable period of flight, were it linear in nature. The eight second observable period of flight spanned approximately 6.7 degrees of circular flight and between 38 and 44.7 degrees of orientation. The 122 through 134 foot drift estimates are based on the aircraft bearings of 38 and 44.7 degrees respectively.

III Higher Speeds Limit Lateral Drift and Deflection Angles

For the morning of September 11, 2001, wind speed and direction for the altitude of the aircraft impacts with each WTC tower were reported to be between 11 mph and 22 mph, from the direction of true north.[6] For the analysis at hand, the average estimate of 16.5mph (24.2 f/s) is used. Wind speeds near coastlines like those on Manhattan at the Hudson River and Upper New York Bay, can often be double those recorded inland, creating a less predictable guidance environment. Wind directions near such coastlines are also known to be less predictable than inland winds.[7] The north faces of each WTC tower were oriented 29 degrees clockwise from true north.[8] The impact of AA 11 with WTC 1 was perpendicular to its north face. The impact of UA 175 was approximately 9 degrees clockwise of perpendicular to its south face.

Comparison of observed higher and hypothesized lower aircraft speeds demonstrates that the greater observed speed of UA 175 reduced potential wind induced drift angles and ground track drift distances while enroute toward WTC 2.

At its time of impact with WTC 1, AA 11 is estimated to have been traveling at a speed of 683f/s (466 mph).[9] At its time of impact with WTC 2, UA 175 is estimated to have been traveling at a speed of 799f/s (545 mph).[10] Adjusted hypothetical speeds for AA 11 and UA 175 (185 mph or 272f/s) used for the following comparison to the observed aircraft speeds, are based on recommended wide-body commercial aviation aircraft landing approach speeds.[11]

Lateral displacement per 1,000 feet traveled for UA 175, while traveling at 799 f/s, is just 19.15 feet ([1,000/799f/s] x 15.3f/s = 19.15). However, displacement per 1,000 feet traveled for UA 175 if traveling at 272 f/s is 55.15 feet ([1,000/272f/s] x 15f/s = 55.15).

Lateral displacement per 1,000 feet traveled for AA 11, while traveling at 683 f/s, is just 17.42 feet ([1,000/683f/s] x 11.9f/s = 17.42). However, displacement per 1,000 feet traveled for AA 11 if traveling at 272 f/s is 43.4 feet ([1,000/272f/s] x 11.8f/s = 43.38).

Illustration Based on CBS Video Footage Depicting UA 175's Final 13 Seconds of Flight

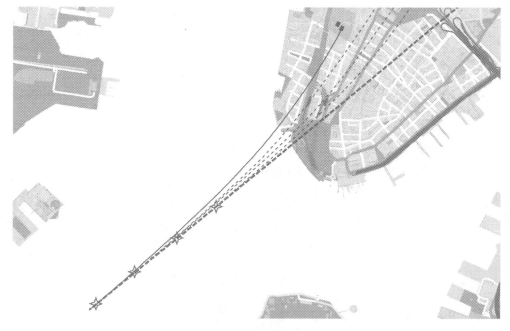

Illustration of UA 175 One Second Turn Delay Increments and Corresponding Target Miss Distances

As demonstrated, the extraordinarily high speeds of the aircraft that impacted the WTC towers, would help to preserve their intended courses based on distances traveled while enroute to their targets, by minimizing deflection angles and ground track displacements created by present crosswinds and potential wind shear.

Achieving a desired course under crosswind conditions that can deflect an aircraft from a desired destination, requires consideration of the relationship between an aircraft's direction and speed, with respect to a wind's direction and speed.

Such relationships are represented trigonometrically by a "wind triangle", which is typically calculated by aircraft FMSs:

> On aircraft equipped with advanced navigation equipment, the wind triangle is often solved within the flight management system, (FMS) using inputs from the air data computer (ADC), inertial navigation system (INS), global positioning system (GPS), and other instruments, (VOR), (DME), (ADF).[12]

Although human control of UA 175 cannot be ruled out, small margins for error are evident in the number of available degrees of bank that could generate impact with WTC 2, via a constant radius turn from approximately 1.5 miles distant. An error of just 5 degrees of bank left or right seems largely indiscernible to an observer, but would generate substantial and accumulating error distances from a given target. To achieve impact via a mile-long plus, constant radius banked turn within an acceptable margin of error, would seem to be a substantial challenge to a reportedly inexperienced pilot without aid. The CWS function would apparently provide an in-flight automated stability that would permit a pilot to apply greater attention to the course of an aircraft and consider whether additional maneuvers would be required. However, success would require an ability to simultaneously and precisely estimate a correct turn start time and calculate crosswind effect potential.

In contrast to the observed controlled flight of UA 175 during the seconds before its impact with WTC 2, it has been posited by some that because NTSB FDR information indicates inexperienced human control of AA 77, in the form of repeated and erratic changes in aircraft altitude, attitude, speed and direction, that therefore human control of the other three aircraft destroyed on September 11, 2001 is more likely.

Yet as mentioned, discrepancies surrounding the authenticity and quality of this FDR data are public knowledge. These would include the absence of published inventory control serial numbers for the FDRs of AA 77 and UA 93 and a discrepancy of 5 hours between the reported recovery time of AA 77's alleged FDR and the time stamp contained within its data download file. [13] [14]

The CWS autopilot feature described earlier as being capable of maintaining the stable 20 degree bank angle observed during UA 175's mile-plus long approach toward WTC 2, was apparently a standard feature of Boeing 767-200s circa 2001.[15] However, photographic flight deck evidence suggests the CWS feature within American Airlines and United Airlines 767s was disabled circa 2001.[16][17]

However, adjustable autopilot bank angle limitations discussed earlier are seemingly one aspect of modifiable aircraft performance related FMS default settings, contained within easily loadable FMS software:

> Many newer airplanes, such as the Boeing . . . 767, feature loadable systems whose functionality may be changed or updated using onboard loadable software. This feature allows operators to change the configuration of loadable systems without physically modifying or replacing hardware components. In addition, software often can be loaded just in the time required to turn an airplane around for the next flight. Some of the databases used by software loadable LRUs (line replaceable units) are: Flight management computer (FMC) navigation database (NDB); FMC performance defaults database.[18]

When considering the probability of conventional autopilot and CWS control of UA 175, the uniformity and accuracy of the initial bank angle capable of causing impact from approximately 1.5 miles away, weighs against CWS facilitated human control, as it indicates that the initial bank angle was set very accurately. The low probability of such a fortunate initial bank angle selection is remarkable. Given the multiple variables to be weighed by a human pilot achieving a well centered impact with WTC 2 from over 1.5 miles distant via a constant radius turn, manual or CWS assisted terrorist control of UA 175 seems unlikely.

6. Misdirection at the Pentagon?

At 8:57am on September 11, 2001, AA 77 fails to respond to routine communications with the Indianapolis ATC center [1]. By this time AA 11 and UA 175 have crashed into the twin towers of the WTC in New York City and an escalating national airspace emergency is already underway. In quick succession, AA 77 first veers off its planned course near the Ohio and West Virginia border and then ceases providing a primary radar return and then secondary radar flight information to ATC via its transponder, creating a subsequent impression that its flight deck has also been taken over as is alleged to be the case with AA 11 and UA 175. After ten minutes, AA 77 then suddenly reappears but is not immediately noticed by ATC [2]. Five minutes later it enters airspace managed by Washington ATC [3].

Precisely what unfolds between this time and the moment of AA 77's reported impact with the Pentagon has become a matter of intensive speculation and debate. It would seem that based on all available evidence that an American Airlines 757 crashed into the E ring of the west side of the Pentagon at 9:37am. However, skeptics cannot necessarily be faulted for questions raised by what is seemingly an unusually small impact hole reportedly created by the plane's collision with the building's E ring, as well as the reported aircraft wreckage exit hole from within the Pentagon's C ring located deeper within the building. Yet these questions are not satisfactorily answered by the virtually unsupported claims by certain parties that a missile or other type of smaller aircraft was responsible for this damage.

Official accounts based on FDR data recreations and on scene physical flight path damage evidence portray AA 77 just moments before its reported Pentagon impact as traveling several hundred feet to the south of the U.S. Navy Annex building (located several thousand feet to the west of the Pentagon) and also just south of the then Citgo gas station located just between the Pentagon and Navy Annex buildings. (See Chapter 7 illustrations) These landmarks will figure prominently in the debate that has ensued since the 2006 AA 77 event eyewitness interviews recorded on scene at the vicinity of the Pentagon by determined independent researchers. And while these researchers have drawn conclusions from the information they obtained that may prove incorrect, these accounts have seemingly also provided the circumstantial evidence leading one to much less obvious but perhaps most plausible and remarkable of all possible event outcomes.

I Fifth Anniversary Pentagon Witness Interviews

At approximately the time of the fifth anniversary of the September 11 attacks, two amateur California researchers were able to audio and video record the recollections of nearly a dozen subjects who witnessed virtually all of the events surrounding the final seconds of flight of AA 77 while upon other properties just adjacent to the Pentagon [4].

Overhead View of Official and Various Observed AA 77 Flight Paths Toward Pentagon

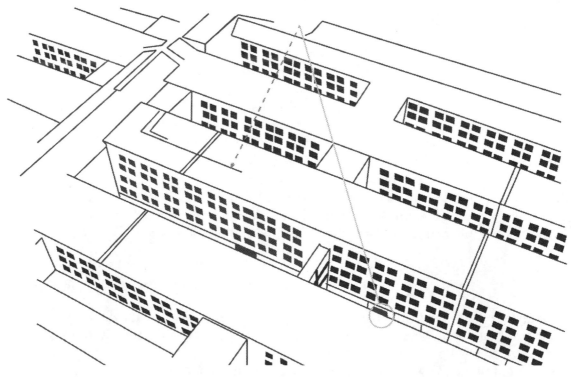

Official AA 77 Impact Path (Solid Line) Toward C-Ring "Punch-Out" Hole and Projected Impact Path (Dashed Line) Via "North of Citgo" Route

While these subjects previously provided their official accounts to other parties, these latest 2006 interviews were able to extract flight path details for AA 77 not provided within the earlier accounts, that while at first seem less than significant, are in fact upon closer examination seemingly fatal to the official version of events for AA 77.

Of this witness group, the most important are three who were located at the then Citgo gas station at 9:37am on September 11, 2001. These were a station employee Robert Turcious and two uniformed Pentagon Police officers William LaGasse and Chadwick Brooks. All three reported that AA 77 flew past their location to the north of the Citgo gas station. The station was located approximately one thousand feet to the west of the Pentagon. However, FDR recreations, downed street light posts and a reportedly damaged construction power generator trailer just outside of the Pentagon suggest AA 77 traveling a low and fast route hundreds of feet to the south of the Citgo station seconds before its reported crash. The said Citgo accounts are seemingly corroborated by the accounts of interviewed Arlington Cemetery employees located approximately one thousand feet to the north of the Citgo station and by others to the west of Citgo.

Are these three remarkable recollections simply mistaken? It would seem unlikely. One witness was an employee of the Citgo station and quite familiar with the property. The other two were law enforcement officers who frequented the station and are expert with respect to observing and reporting events. In addition, although they were located upon different parts of the Citgo property at the time AA 77 flew past, both LaGasse and Brooks provided remarkably similar hand drawn illustrations of AA 77's flight path upon aerial photos of the vicinity, which were created during the interviews.

Just over one thousand feet further west of the Citgo station are witnesses Terry Morin and Edward Paik. Morin seemingly reports AA 77 as flying over his location at the southern edge of the Navy Annex building, which is hundreds of feet further north than the flight path depicted by alleged FDR data and that required to create the physical damage to Pentagon property light posts and portable power generators reportedly struck by AA 77 milliseconds before its Pentagon collision. Several hundred feet west of Morin's location is where Paik seemingly reports AA 77 as flying nearly above and just slightly to the south of his automotive repair business, which is also hundreds of feet further north than the FDR path and that required to create the said property damage.

As a result of these highly corroborating accounts contradicting official flight path claims, one can rightly and reasonably question the authenticity of the said FDR data and physical evidence relied upon to support such claims regarding AA 77's route just before its reported collision with the Pentagon. However, any charges of evidence falsification would do well to also be supported by at least plausible motives for any official deception.

II C Ring Exit Hole FDR Recovery Site

According to official accounts, following the impact with the Pentagon's outer E ring, the disintegrated remains of AA 77 continued into the building another three hundred feet and eventually penetrated the eastern wall of its so called C ring, spilling what is alleged to be just a tiny fraction of the Boeing 757's airframe into a courtyard area. Just inside this hole is where only the plane's front landing gear and FDR - interestingly installed into the very rear of the aircraft - were reportedly recovered. Shouldn't much of the 130,000 pound 757 airframe have thus also been present at the C ring exit hole location? Images of this hole in the immediate aftermath of its reported creation oddly suggest this was not the case.

The dimensions of this curiously well-defined and unexpectedly compact hole within a brick wall, located hundreds of feet beyond the Pentagon E ring impact point, were less than ten feet in diameter.

Could just small amounts of dispersed and lightweight fragments of a disintegrated aluminum airframe retain enough explosive energy required to create such a compact hole, which also just happens to bear a strong resemblance to those holes that are also created by explosive military rapid wall breaching kits? [5] Is it also just a coincidence that the sound of an unseen second powerful blast was captured live during local television coverage just in front of the Pentagon, which was comparable in magnitude to those generated by the said wall breaching kits during video demonstrations? [6]

III A Motive for Deception?

Should it be the case that certain Pentagon disaster scene evidence was in fact manipulated by unknown parties in such a way as to create an impression of a false impact trajectory, one is left to wonder what could be gained by any perpetrators of such activity? By recalling that reportedly recovered FDR data for AA 77 and UA 93 was primary evidence cited by authorities of accused hijacker flight deck takeovers and that the authenticity of this data is seemingly suspect, one is caused to consider that the suspect C ring hole and the problematic impact trajectory alleged to have created it, were instead both fabricated in order to ensure that unknown parties could introduce an easily recoverable false FDR within the Pentagon disaster scene.

Would federal concealment of dozens of Pentagon property videos potentially capturing AA 77's reported impact with the Pentagon, have been done so in order to in fact conceal the plane's true flight path toward the building? [7] Some have alleged with virtually no supporting evidence that an American Airlines 757 didn't collide with the Pentagon on September 11 and that for this reason, such said videos have been withheld from public view.

However, these points of view are apparently contradicted by ATC professionals within nearby Reagan International Airport's control tower, who were monitoring AA 77's approach toward the Pentagon and who claimed to witness the plane's eventual collision with the building. [8]

Little of FBI and NTSB recovery results of AA 77's 130,000 pounds of wreckage or passenger remains is known, beyond just several images of aircraft landing gear and engine components within the Pentagon and an American Society of Civil Engineers (ASCE) Pentagon Building Performance Report diagram of where passenger remains were reportedly recovered along the alleged path of AA 77 through the building following impact [9]. Presumably, this alleged remains recovery information was provided to the ASCE by the FBI, yet requests by the author for corroborating source records for this information requested under the FOIA were oddly refused.

Closer examination of aerial images of the Pentagon following AA77's reported impact in fact suggest a damage pattern more consistent with what has been referred to as a "north of Citgo" (NoC) approach path, more so than the plane's officially reported path.

Such damage would include massive structural failure and fire damage along the said NoC path. This NoC path angle at impact differs from the official path by approximately 45 degrees.

7. Conclusion

If the September 11 attacks prove nothing else, they prove that the major media's idea of investigative journalism is simply reporting federal government press releases as fact. As shown, the official version of September 11 events is little more than basic allegations morphed into fact by media repetition. This fact raises the larger question about the true purpose of America's multi-billion dollar media industry within society.

Yet the attacks also prove that the most significant consequence of the FBI's alleged investigation of September 11 events, is their total seizure of and control over all September 11 evidence and the public's inability to verify details of the most significant event of this century. If the September 11 attacks are the subject of the largest FBI investigation on record and if the guilt of the accused is a settled matter, why is so little documentation surrounding aspects of the event available?

Perhaps this fact is less surprising given recent reports that open records requests of the DoD for images and information related to the reported mission to kill accused September 11 accomplice Osama Bin Laden, have been met by reports that no records were located. [1] Have government records of the greatest significance been segregated beyond the jurisdiction of open records laws?

In 2011, it was reported that the DoJ sought to permit agencies to deny the existence of records requested under the FOIA.[2] Such denials of records existence would allow an agency to avoid the obligation of providing records descriptions within a *Vaughn Index* during litigation. However, such practices seem to be in evidence prior to this DoJ proposal. As noted, the DoJ provided the following suspect reason during 2008 litigation with the author to support their dubious claim that important September 11 records could not be located. The DoJ later advised the author these and other September 11 records that would corroborate key aspects of the official version of September 11 events, would require a remarkable 150 years to release under the FOIA.

> The case agent stated that since the identities of the four hijacked aircraft have never been in question by the FBI, NTSB or FAA (evidence collected after September 11, 2001 has corroborated the fact that American Airlines Flight 11, United Airlines Flight 175, American Airlines Flight 77 and United Flight 93 were the aircraft hijacked), no records would have been generated responsive to plaintiffs request for documents.

Nevertheless, even if it may be the case that government agencies purposely withhold information from the public, the works presented here demonstrate that the most important information regarding some matters may simply be hidden in plain view and waiting to be reported.

U.S. Department of Justice

United States Attorney's Office
District of Nevada

Gregory A. Brower
United States Attorney

333 Las Vegas Boulevard South   *Phone (702) 388-6336*
Suite 5000   *Fax (702) 388-6296*
Las Vegas, Nevada 89101

June 16, 2009

Via Federal Express

Aidan Monaghan
████████████████████
Las Vegas, NV ████████

Re: *Aidan Monaghan v. Department of Justice,* case no. 2:09-cv-00608-KJD-LRL

Dear Mr. Monaghan:

I would like to speak with you concerning the requests for information that are at issue in this lawsuit. I write this letter pursuant to Federal Rule of Civil Procedure 408 in an effort to resolve this lawsuit, and neither this letter nor any related statements are admissible in court.

The first request (or sub-request) in the lawsuit is for "records generated or obtained regarding the FBI investigation of the 4 aircraft hijacked and destroyed at the World Trade Center in New York city, NY, the Pentagon building in Arlington, VA and Shanksville, PA during the terrorist attacks of September 11, 2001." This appears to be a request for all records from the FBI's investigative file for the September 11, 2001 terrorist attacks. As a request for all records, it would encompass your other requests (or sub-requests). For purposes of this letter, I will put aside for the moment the categorical exemptions from disclosure for various materials in that file.

As I am sure you can appreciate, the FBI's investigative file on the significant and horrific events of September 11, 2001 is extremely large. Indeed, it is so large that the FBI conservatively estimates it would take well over 150 years to process your request for records from the investigative file (the FBI currently processes approximately 600 pages per month, or 7,200 pages per year, in responding to various FOIA requests). I would note that this estimate is simply for the processing and release of any information and does not include administrative preparation for the processing which will be extraordinarily time-consuming. Likewise, the fees for processing such an enormous request as yours would also be significant.

It is also my understanding that certain information has already been provided to you either directly or through reference to certain web sites or other sources of public information.

Department of Justice Correspondence (2009)

Appendix

Turn Calculations for AA 11 and UA 175

Estimates for aircraft turn radius and turn circumference are derived from the following calculations:

Aircraft turn radiuses (r) are provided by: $r = $ true airspeed^2/32.16 [tan(angle of bank)].
Aircraft turn circumferences (c) are provided by: $c = 2(Pi)r$.

The proportions of each constant radius turn completed are provided by:

Turn arc time = (speed)(time/circumference of turn).

Turn proportions are then multiplied by 360° to determine the number of degrees of each turn completed:

UA 175's Final Turn radius (Aircraft A) = 799^2/32.16(tan)(29°) = 35,813 feet.

This 29°AoB is an approximated average for a span of 20°-38° during the 2.5 seconds prior to impact with WTC 2 [38-20=18; 18/2=9; 20+9=29].

UA 175's Final Turn angle: [(799f/s)2.5/225,020] 360 = 3.196° of turn.
UA 175's Next-to-Final Turn radius (Aircraft B) = 799^2/32.16(tan)(20°) = 54,541 feet.

This 20°AoB is based on observed approximations.

UA 175's Next-to-Final Turn angle: [(799f/s)2.5/342,691] 360 = 2.098° of turn.

Angles of turn completed and turn radiuses are then utilized in order to obtain ordered pairs for use in a Cartesian coordinate system:

X(for Turns A and B) = r - [(r)(cos)(degrees of turn)] Y(for Turns A and B) = (r)(sin)(degrees of turn)

Aircraft Turn A (final turn):

Xa = 35,813 - [35,813 (cos3.196)] = 55.701 Ya = [35,813 (sin3.196)] = 1,996.639

Aircraft Turn B (next-to-final turn):

$Xb = 54,541 - [54,541 (\cos 2.098)] = 36.560$ $Yb = [54,541(\sin 2.098)] = 1,996.681$

Individual aircraft X and Y components are combined:

X-separation = Xa - Xb $\quad$ Y-separation = Ya - Yb

X-separation = $55.701 - 36.560 = 19.141$; Y-separation = $1,996.639 - 1,996.681 = -.042$

The approximate final distance between UA 175's next-to-final turn and its final turn at impact with WTC 2, is obtained by Pythagorean's theorem:

$[(\text{X-separation}^2) + (\text{Y-separation}^2)] = 19.141^2 + -.042^2 = 366.379 \ ^{1/2} = 19.141$ feet.

Vector Calculations for American Airlines Flight 11

P (plane): approximate compass bearing 209° (traveling approximately southwest) at 662 f/s (446 mph air speed); W (wind): traveling south at 24.2 f/s (16.5 mph).

Plane and wind vector components represented by ordered pairs:

$P = [662 \text{ f/s } \cos(241°), 662 \text{ f/s } \sin(241°)] = -320.9, -579$
$W = [24.2 \text{ f/s } \cos(270°), 24.2 \text{ f/s } \sin(270°)] = 0, -24.2$
$[(-320.9) + 0] = -320.9; [(-579) + (-24.2)] = -603.2$

Resolved components substituted into Pythagoreans theorem for resultant speed:

$\|P + W\| = 320.9^2 + 603.2^2 = 466, 827 \ ^{1/2} = 683.2$ f/s (466 mph ground speed)

Resolved components substituted for resultant bearing:

$\tan^{-1}(603.2/320.9) = 62°$; $(90° - 62°) + 180° = 208°$
Drift angle = 209° - 208° = 1°
Ground track displacement = 1°tan(683f/s) = 11.9f/s

Vector Calculations for Adjusted Speed for American Airlines Flight 11

P (plane): approximate compass bearing 209° (traveling approximately southwest) at 272 f/s (185 mph air speed); W (wind): traveling south at 24.2 f/s (16.5 mph).

Plane and wind vector components represented by ordered pairs:

P = [272 f/s cos(241°), 272 f/s sin(241°)] = -131.9, -237.9
W = [24.2 f/s cos(270°), 24.2 f/s sin(270°)] = 0, -24.2
[(-131.9) + 0] = -131.9; [(-237.9) + (-24.2)] = -262.1

Resolved components substituted into Pythagoreans theorem for resultant speed:

$\|P + W\|$ = 131.9² + 262.1² = 86,094 ¹ᐟ² = 293.4 f/s (205 mph ground speed)

Resolved components substituted for resultant bearing:

tan ⁻¹(262.1/131.9) = 63.3°; (90° - 63.3°) + 180° = 206.7°
Drift angle = 209° - 206.7° = 2.3°
Ground track displacement = 2.3°tan(293.4 f/s) = 11.8 f/s

Vector Calculations for United Airlines Flight 175

P (plane): approximate compass bearing 38° (traveling approximately northeast) at 818 f/s (561 mph air speed); W (wind): traveling south at 24.2 f/s (16.5 mph).

Plane and wind vector components represented by ordered pairs:

P = [818 f/s cos(52°), 818 f/s sin(52°)] = 503.6, 644.6
W = [24.2 f/s cos(270°), 24.2 f/s sin(270°)] = 0, -24.2
[503.6 + 0] = 503.6; [644.6 + (-24.2)] = 620.4

Resolved components substituted into Pythagoreans theorem for resultant speed:

$\|P + W\|$ = 503.6² + 620.4² = 638,509 ¹ᐟ² = 799 f/s (545 mph ground speed)

Resolved components substituted for resultant bearing:

tan ⁻¹(620.4/503.6) = 50.9°; (90° - 50.9°) = 39.1°
Drift angle = 39.1° - 38° = 1.1°
Ground track displacement = 1.1°tan(799 f/s) = 15.3f/s

Vector Calculations for Adjusted Speed for United Airlines Flight 175

P (plane): approximate compass bearing 38° (traveling approximately northeast) at speed 272 f/s (185 mph air speed); W (wind): traveling south at 24.2 f/s (16.5 mph).

Plane and wind vector components represented by ordered pairs:

P = [272 f/s cos(52°), 272 f/s sin(52°)] = 167.4, 214.3
W = [24.2 f/s cos(270°), 24.2 f/s sin(270°)] = 0, -24.2
[167.4 + 0] = 167.4; [214.3 + (-24.2)] = 190.1

Resolved components substituted into Pythagoreans theorem for resultant speed:

$\|P + W\| = 167.4^2 + 190.1^2 = 64,160^{1/2} = 253.3$ f/s (168 mph ground speed)

Resolved components substituted for resultant bearing:

$\tan^{-1}(190.1/167.4) = 48.6°$; (90° - 48.6°) = 41.4°
Drift angle = 41.4° - 38° = 3.4°
Ground track displacement = 3.4°tan(253.3 f/s) = 15 f/s

UA 175 Turn Separation Between 15 and 20 Degrees of Bank

Aircraft Turn A: 15°: (r: 74,086); [(799)(8/465,496)](360) = 4.943
Aircraft Turn B: 20°: (r: 54,540); [(799)(8/342,685)](360) = 6.715

Aircraft Turn A:

X_a (15°) = 74,086 - [74,086 (cos)(4.943)] = 275.532 Y_a (15°) = 74,086 (sin)(4.943) = 6,383.594

Aircraft Turn B:

X_b (20°) = 54,540 - [54,540(cos)(6.715)] = 374.140 Y_b (20°) = 54,540 (sin)(6.715) = 6,377.402

X-separation = X_a - X_b Y-separation = Y_a - Y_b

X-separation = 275.532 - 374.140 = -98.608 Y-separation = 6,383.594 - 6,377.402= 6.192

Separation = square root of [(X-separation^2) + (Y-separation^2)]

$(-98.608)^2 + (6.192)^2 = 9,752.595^{1/2} = 98.802$ feet

UA 175 Turn Separation Between 20 and 25 Degrees of Bank

Aircraft Turn A: 20°: (r: 54,540); [(799)(8/342,685)](360) = 6.714
Aircraft Turn B: 25°: (r: 42,571); [(799)(8/267,481)](360) = 8.602

Aircraft Turn A:

Xa (20°) = 54,540 - [(54,540)(cos)(6.715)] = 374.140 Ya (20°) = 54,540(sin)(6.715) = 6,377.402

Aircraft Turn B:

Xb (25°) = 42,571 - [(42,571)(cos)(8.602)] = 478.874 Yb (25°) = 42,571(sin)(8.602) = 6,367.338

X-separation = Xa - Xb Y-separation = Ya - Yb

X-separation = 374.140 - 478.874 = -104.734 Y-separation = 6,377.402 - 6,367.338 = 10.06

Separation = square root of [(X-separation^2) + (Y-separation^2)]

$(-104.734)^2 + (10.06)^2 = 11,075.630^{1/2} = 105.216$ feet

Notes

Introduction

[1] *9:59 a.m. September 11, 2001: Some Witnesses Hear Explosions as South Tower Collapses*
http://www.historycommons.org/context.jsp?item=a959hearexplosions#a959hearexplosions

[2] *10:28 a.m. September 11, 2001: Some Witnesses Hear Explosions as North Tower Collapses*
http://www.historycommons.org/context.jsp?item=a1028explosionsheard#a1028explosionsheard

[3] *The "Deep Mystery" of Melted Steel*
http://www.wpi.edu/News/Transformations/2002Spring/steel.html

[4] *Engineers are baffled over the collapse of 7 WTC; Steel members have been partly evaporated*
James Glanz, New York Times, November 29. 2001

[5] *Stabilized WTC Molten Metal*
http://www.youtube.com/watch?v=IA3gHjg7c-E

[6] *September 12, 2001-February 2002: Witnesses See Molten Metal in the Remains at Ground Zero*
http://www.historycommons.org/context.jsp?item=a091201moltenmetal#a091201moltenmetal

[7] *Why Indeed Did the WTC Buildings Completely Collapse?*
http://www.journalof911studies.com/volume/200609/Why_Indeed_Did_the_WTC_Buildings_Completely_Collapse_Jones_Thermite_World_Trade_Center.pdf

[8] *DMB1 Airlines FDR - Letters From Condon Forsyth LLP Re American Airlines Document Requests*
http://www.scribd.com/doc/15492358/DM-B1-Airlines-Fdr-Letters-From-Condon-Forsyth-LLP-Re-American-Airlines-Document-Requests

Chapter 1

[1] *Terror Devastates A/E/C Firms*
http://www.highbeam.com/doc/1G1-79439506.html

[2] *Port Authority of NY/NJ: Records For Reported WTC Renovation Work Destroyed On 9/11*
http://911blogger.com/news/2009-04-21/port-authority-nynj-records-reported-wtc-renovation-work-destroyed-911

[3] *Naval Surface Warfare Center at Indian Head Mourns Loss of Its Energetic Champion*
http://www.highbeam.com/doc/1P2-574412.html

[4] *Active Thermitic Material Discovered in Dust from the 9/11 World Trade Center Catastrophe*
http://www.benthamscience.com/open/tocpj/articles/V002/7TOCPJ.htm?TOCPJ/2009/00000002/00000001/7TOCPJ.SGM

[5] *Turner Corporation 1997 10-K Report*
http://www.buck.com/10k?tenkyear=97&idx=T&co=!TURNERC&nam=DEMO2&pw=DEMO2

[6] *The Top Ten Connections Between NIST and Nano-Thermites*
http://www.journalof911studies.com/volume/2008/Ryan_NIST_and_Nano-1.pdf

[7] *Kingdome – GUINNESS WORLD RECORD!! – Controlled Demolition, Inc.*
http://www.dubaiburj.com/kingdome-guinness-world-record-controlled-demolition-inc/

[8] *Is Dome's demise a date with fate?*
http://seattlepi.nwsource.com/local/dome04.shtml

[9] *Another amazing coincidence related to the WTC*
     http://www.911blogger.com/node/13272

[10] *Additional Port Authority Of NY/NJ WTC Property Assessment FOI Records*
     http://911blogger.com/news/2009-11-04/additional-port-authority-nynj-wtc-property-assessment-foi-records

[11] *Lend Lease secures contract to manage Ground Zero clean-up*
     http://www.highbeam.com/doc/1G1-81303508.html

[12] *Thomas C. Leppert Named To Succeed E.T. Gravette, Jr. As Chairman Of The Turner Corporation*
     http://www.turnerconstruction.com/corporate/content.asp?d=1222&p=1153

[13] *TomLeppert.com*
     http://www.tomleppert.com/PR/docs/fellows_commission.pdf

[14] *Mayor Leppert meets with Bush*
     http://www.bizjournals.com/dallas/stories/2008/01/21/daily26.html

[15] *DRIVE TO THE TOP*
     http://www.elevator-world.com/magazine/archive01/0103-002.html-ssi

[16] *The Buildings Information System*
     http://www.nyc.gov/html/dob/html/bis/bis.shtml

[17] *Elevators*
     http://www.nyc.gov/html/dob/html/applications_and_permits/elevator_home . . . .

[18] *Elevators: Applications and Permits*
     http://www.nyc.gov/html/dob/html/applications_and_permits/elevator_appl . . . .

[19] *REFERENCE MATERIALS: 1968 New York City Building Code*
     http://www.nyc.gov/html/dob/html/reference/code_internet.shtml

[20] *TRIMMING THE BUSHES—Family Business at the Watergate*
     http://www.washingtonspectator.org/articles/20050215bushes_1.ctm

Chapter 2

[1] *UPDATE: U.S. BTS FOIA Records For 9/11 Planes Differ From BTS Online Database*
     http://911blogger.com/news/2009-06-22/update-us-bts-foia-records-911-planes-differ-bts-online-database

[2] *UPDATE: U.S. BTS FOIA Records For 9/11 Planes Differ From BTS Online Database*
     http://911blogger.com/news/2009-06-22/update-us-bts-foia-records-911-planes-differ-bts-online-database

[3] *UPDATE: U.S. BTS FOIA Records For 9/11 Planes Differ From BTS Online Database*
     http://911blogger.com/news/2009-06-22/update-us-bts-foia-records-911-planes-differ-bts-online-database

[4] *FBI Records Chief Describes Unsuccessful Search For Identifying Records Of 9/11 Aircraft Wreckage & Flight
     Data Recorders*
     http://911blogger.com/news/2008-08-27/fbi-records-chief-describes-unsuccessful-search-identifying-records-
     911-aircraft-wreckage-flight-data-recorders

[5] *Airborne Anti-Terrorist Operation Getting Underway*
     http://edition.cnn.com/TRANSCRIPTS/0206/04/lt.08.html

[6] *Capstone Safety Engineering Report #1*
     http://adsb.tc.faa.gov/RFG/Capstone%20I%20PHA%20Vol%201%202000-12-02.pdf

[7] *NORAD Exercises-Hijack Summary-Commission Sensitive*
     http://www.scribd.com/doc/81542105/NORAD-Hijack-Exercises

[8] *FBI Records Chief Describes Unsuccessful Search For Identifying Records Of 9/11 Aircraft Wreckage & Flight
     Data Recorders*
     http://911blogger.com/news/2008-08-27/fbi-records-chief-describes-unsuccessful-search-identifying-records-
     911-aircraft-wreckage-flight-data-recorders

[9]   *NTSB: No Records Pertaining To Process Of Positive Identification Of 9/11 Aircraft Wreckage*
      http://911blogger.com/news/2008-07-23/ntsb-no-records-pertaining-process-positive-identification-911-aircraft-wreckage

[10] *Remarks of Carol Carmody Vice-Chairman, National Transportation Safety Board Leadership in Times of Crisis Seminar*
      http://www.ntsb.gov/speeches/carmody/cc020227.htm

[11] *Testimony of Marion C. Blakey, Chairman National Transportation Safety Board before the Committee on Commerce, Science and Transportation United States Senate*
      http://www.ntsb.gov/Speeches/blakey/mcb020625.htm

[12] *Freedom of Information Act (FOIA) Exemptions*
      http://www.faa.gov/foia/media/exemptions.pdf

[13] *9/11 Aircraft 'Black Box' Serial Numbers Mysteriously Absent*
      http://911blogger.com/news/2008-02-26/911-aircraft-black-box-serial-numbers-mysteriously-absent

[14] Comair Flight 5191, August 27, 2006, CRJ-100, 49 Dead, Fairchild Model F-1000 FDR, Serial Number: 102368
      http://www.ntsb.gov/publictn/2007/AAR0705.pdf

[15] Chalk's Ocean Airways Flight 101, December 19, 2005, Grumman G-73, 20 Dead (Not equipped with a FDR)
      http://amelia.db.erau.edu/reports/ntsb/aar/AAR07-04.pdf

[16] Corporate Airlines Flight 5966, October 19, 2004, HP Jetstream, 13 Dead, Fairchild Model F-1000 FDR, Serial Number: 00511
      http://www.ntsb.gov/publictn/2006/AAR0601.pdf

[17] Pinnacle Airlines Flight 3701, October 14, 2004, CL-600-2B19, 2 Dead, Fairchild Model F-1000 FDR, Serial Model: 01094
      http://www.ntsb.gov/publictn/2007/AAR0701.pdf

[18] US Airways Express Flight 5481, January 8, 2003, Beechcraft 1900, 21 Dead, Fairchild Model F-1000 FDR, Serial Number: 01110
      http://www.ntsb.gov/events/2003/AM5481/docket/255651.pdf

[19] American Airlines Flight 587, November 12, 2001, Airbus 300, 260 Dead, Fairchild Model FA-2100 FDR, Serial Number: 1186
      http://www.ntsb.gov/Events/2001/AA587/exhibits/241509.pdf

[20] Alaska Airlines Flight 261, January 31, 2000, Boeing MD-83, 88 Dead, Sundstrand Model FDR, Serial Number: 9182
      http://www.ntsb.gov/Events/2000/Aka261/docket/117973.pdf

[21] American Airlines Flight 1420, June 1, 1999, McDonnell Douglas MD-82, 11 Dead, L3 Model FA-2100 FDR, Serial Number: 00718
      http://www.ntsb.gov/publictn/2001/AAR0102.pdf

[22] COMAIR Flight 3272, January 9, 1997, Empresa Brasileira de Aeronautica, 29 Dead, Loral Fairchild Model F-1000 FDR, Serial Number: 997
      http://www.ntsb.gov/publictn/1998/AAR9804_body.pdf

[23] TWA Flight 800, July 17, 1996, Boeing 747, 230 Dead, Sundstrand Model FDR, Serial Number: 10291
      http://www.ntsb.gov/Publictn/2000/AAR0003.pdf

[24] Valu Jet Flight 592, May 11, 1996, McDonnell Douglas DC-9, 110 Dead, Loral Fairchild Model F-800 FDR, Serial Number: 6132
      http://www.ntsb.gov/Publictn/1997/AAR9706.pdf

[25] Atlantic Southeast Airlines Flight 529, August 21, 1995, EMB-120RT, 8 Dead, Fairchild Digital Model F-800 FDR, Serial Number: 04856
http://www.ntsb.gov/publictn/1996/AAR9606.pdf

[26] American Eagle Flight 4184, October 31, 1994, ATR 72, 68 Dead, Loral/Fairchild Model F-800 FDR, Serial Number: 4838
http://www.ntsb.gov/Publictn/1996/aar9601.pdf

[27] US Air Flight 427, September 8, 1994, Boeing 737-300, 133 Dead, Loral/Fairchild Data Systems Model F-1000 FDR, Serial Number: 442
http://www.ntsb.gov/publictn/1999/AAR9901.pdf

[28] US Air Flight 1016, July 2, 1994, McDonnell Douglas DC-9, 37 Dead, Fairchild S-703 FDR, Serial Number: 00880
http://amelia.db.erau.edu/reports/ntsb/aar/AAR95-03.pdf

[29] US Air Flight 405, March 22, 1992, Fokker F-28, 27 Dead, Fairchild F-800 FDR, Serial Number: 154
http://www.airdisaster.com/reports/ntsb/AAR93-02.pdf

[30] Atlantic Southeast Airlines Flight 2311, April 5, 1991, Embraer EMB 120, 23 Dead, (Not equipped with a FDR)
http://amelia.db.erau.edu/reports/ntsb/aar/AAR92-03.pdf

[31] United Airlines Flight 585, March 3, 1991, Boeing 737, 25 Dead, Fairchild Model F-800 FDR, Serial Number: 4016
http://amelia.db.erau.edu/reports/ntsb/aar/AAR92-06.pdf

[32] US Air Flight 1493, February 1, 1991, Boeing 737, 22 Dead, Sundstrand Model FWUS FDR, Serial Number: 692
http://amelia.db.erau.edu/reports/ntsb/aar/AAR91-08.pdf

[33] United Airlines Flight 232, July 19, 1989, McDonnell Douglas DC 10, 111 Dead, Sundstrand Model 573 FDR, Serial Number: 2159
http://www.airdisaster.com/reports/ntsb/AAR90-06.pdf

[34] Delta Air Lines Flight 1141, August 31, 1988, Boeing 727, 14 Dead, Lockheed Model 109-D, FDR, Serial Number: 654
http://amelia.db.erau.edu/reports/ntsb/aar/AAR89-04.pdf

[35] Continental Express Flight 2574, September 11, 1991, EMB 120, 14 Dead, FDR Manufacturer, Model & Serial Number Not Available.
http://www.airdisaster.com/reports/ntsb/AAR92-04.pdf

[36] *NTSB Describes Importance Of Unpublished 9/11 FDR Part Numbers And Serial Numbers*
http://911blogger.com/news/2008-06-13/ntsb-describes-importance-unpublished-911-fdr-part-numbers-and-serial-numbers

[37] *NTSB Describes Importance Of Unpublished 9/11 FDR Part Numbers And Serial Numbers*
http://911blogger.com/news/2008-06-13/ntsb-describes-importance-unpublished-911-fdr-part-numbers-and-serial-numbers

[38] *Flight Data Recorder Handbook for Aviation Accident Investigations*
http://www.ntsb.gov/doclib/manuals/FDR_Handbook.pdf

[39] *NTSB Describes Importance Of Unpublished 9/11 FDR Part Numbers And Serial Numbers*
http://911blogger.com/news/2008-06-13/ntsb-describes-importance-unpublished-911-fdr-part-numbers-and-serial-numbers

[40] *Pentagon 9/11 Flight 'Black Box' Data File Created Before Actual 'Black Box' Was Recovered*
http://911blogger.com/news/2008-05-18/pentagon-911-flight-black-box-data-file-created-actual-black-box-was-recovered

Chapter 4

[1]   *Global Positioning System.*
http://www.gps.gov/
[2]   *The Making of U.S. Foreign Policy—BIOGRAPHIES OF THE AUTHORS, AMBASSADOR RICHARD LEE ARMITAGE*
http://usinfo.state.gov/journals/itps/0900/ijpe/pj52bios.htm
[3]   *Wide Area Augmentation System.*
http://www.faa.gov/about/office_org/headquarters_offices/ato/service_units/techops/navservices/gnss/waas/howitworks/
[4]   *STATEMENT BY THE PRESIDENT REGARDING THE UNITED STATES' DECISION TO STOP DEGRADING GLOBAL POSITIONING SYSTEM ACCURACY*
http://www.ngs.noaa.gov/FGCS/info/sans_SA/docs/statement.html
[5]   *AMENDED VERSION: Wide Area Augmentation System Signal Now Available*, August 24, 2000
http://www.faa.gov/news/press_releases/news_story.cfm?newsId=5249
[6]   *WAAS Fact Sheet*
http://www.freeflightsystems.com/waas_factsheet.htm
[7]   *DIRECT FLIGHT NEW TECHNOLOGY WILL GUIDE PLANES*
http://www.highbeam.com/doc/1P2-8569182.html
[8]   *WAAS: Back in Step, Avionics Magazine*, February 1, 2002
http://www.aviationtoday.com/av/categories/commercial/12571.html
[9]   *Kent company bringing a navigation revolution*
http://seattletimes.nwsource.com/html/businesstechnology/2003316294_naverus22.html
[10]   *A fuel-saving flight plan*
http://money.cnn.com/galleries/2008/fortune/0807/gallery.copeland_naverus.fortune/index.html
[11]   *DIRECT FLIGHT NEW TECHNOLOGY WILL GUIDE PLANES*
http://www.highbeam.com/doc/1P2-8569182.html
[12]   *Replacing the ILS: the Wide-Area Augmentation System (WAAS) will provide ILS-like accuracy with GPS. Can it replace the familiar ground-based system on which we depend?*
http://www.highbeam.com/doc/1G1-157589720.html
[13]   *UPS wins FAA certification for wide-area GPS receiver*
http://www.flightglobal.com/articles/2003/01/07/159964/ups-wins-faa-certification-for-wide-area-gps-receiver.html
[14]   *RNP Capability of FANS 1 FMCS Equipped 757/767*
http://www.boeing.com/commercial/caft/reference/documents/RNP757767.pdf
[15]   *Kent company bringing a navigation revolution*
http://seattletimes.nwsource.com/html/businesstechnology/2003316294_naverus22.html
[16]   *Air China's First RNP Approach Into Linzhi Airport, Tibet*
http://www.aviationweek.com/aw/generic/story_channel.jsp?channel=comm&id=news/aw092506p1.xml
[17]   *Rockwell Collins To Provide Autoland System for Boeing Next-Generation 737*, Business Wire, October 5, 1999
http://www.highbeam.com/doc/1G1-55993162.html
[18]   *'Automation Addiction': Are Pilots Forgetting How to Fly?*
http://abcnews.go.com/Technology/automation-addiction-pilots-forgetting-fly/story?id=14417730
[19]   *Waypoint*
http://en.wikipedia.org/wiki/Waypoint

[20] *United States Standard For Required Navigation Performance (RNP) Approach Procedures With Special Aircraft And Aircrew Authorization Required (SAAAR)*
http://www.faa.gov/documentLibrary/media/Order/ND/8260_52.pdf

[21] *The International GPS Global Positioning System Waypoint Registry TM*
http://www.waypoint.org/

[22] *FLIGHT MANAGEMENT SYSTEM (FMS) INSTRUMENT PROCEDURES DEVELOPMENT*
http://www.faa.gov/about/office_org/headquarters_offices/avs/offices/afs/afs400/afs420/policies_guidance/orders/media/826040B.pdf

[23] *FLIGHT MANAGEMENT SYSTEM (FMS) INSTRUMENT PROCEDURES DEVELOPMENT*
http://www.faa.gov/about/office_org/headquarters_offices/avs/offices/afs/afs400/afs420/policies_guidance/orders/media/826040B.pdf

[24] *Flight Path Study—American Airlines Flight 77*
http://www.ntsb.gov/info/Flight_%20Path_%20Study_AA77.pdf

[25] *In-flight Demonstrations of Curved Approaches. and Missed Approaches in Mountainous Terrain*
http://waas.stanford.edu/~wwu/jennings/publications/ION98/iongps98.pdf

[26] *Rockwell's Collins Landing System Picked for Both Airbus and Boeing Planes; Lead Announcement at Farnborough Air Show, PRNewswire*, September 6, 1996
http://www.highbeam.com/doc/1G1-18652301.html

[27] *GNSS—Frequently Asked Questions—WAAS*
http://www.faa.gov/about/office_org/headquarters_offices/ato/service_units/techops/navservices/gnss/faq/waas/index.cfm

[28] *Honeywell Announces Orders For New-Generation "Pegasus" Flight Management System, Aviation Week*, September 7, 1998
http://www.aviationnow.com/shownews/farnday1/pressr15.htm

[29] *Boeing 757/767 State of the Art Upgrade*
http://www.honeywell.com/sites/aero/Flight_Management_Systems3_C1997B88E-FCF9-72B5-3A26-801F48F156BD_H79C28D81-B679-A247-C0CE-32B08C84BC08.htm

[30] *Year 2000 Readiness Disclosure (Boeing)*
http://www.boeing.com/commercial/aeromagazine/aero_03/sy/sy01/story.html

[31] *JFK International Airport*
http://upload.wikimedia.org/wikipedia/commons/b/b0/JFK_airport_map.gif

[32] *Chicago-O'Hare International Airport*
http://upload.wikimedia.org/wikipedia/commons/3/30/ORD_airport_map.PNG

[33] *Los Angeles International Airport*
http://upload.wikimedia.org/wikipedia/en/a/a3/LaxAirportDiagram2.jpg

[34] *The World Trade Center*
http://en.wikipedia.org/wiki/File:World_Trade_Center_Building_Design_with_Floor_and_Elevator_Arrangment.svg

[35] *GETTING TO THE POINT IN PINPOINT LANDING*, NASA, 1998
http://www.sti.nasa.gov/tto/spinoff1998/t2.htm

[36] *FAA/Ohio University Avionics Engineering Center Partnership, Federal Aviation Administration*, December, 1998
http://www.tc.faa.gov/logistics/grants/success/OU.pdf

[37] *Honeywell's Differential GPS Satellite Landing System, reprinted from Avionics News Magazine*, September, 1996
http://www.bluecoat.org/reports/Lewison_96_DGPS.pdf

[38] *ARIES: NASA's 'Flying Lab' Takes Wing*
http://oea.larc.nasa.gov/PAIS/757.html

[39] *FAA Performs Successful Satellite-Based Flight Tests Over the North Atlantic*
http://www.faa.gov/news/press_releases/news_story.cfm?newsId=4868

[40] *FAA Completes Successful WAAS Flight Trials in the Republic of Chile*
http://www.faa.gov/news/press_releases/news_story.cfm?newsId=4898

[41] *FAA, ATA, UPS Test New Satellite Technology*, Federal Aviation Administration, August 13, 1999
http://www.faa.gov/news/press_releases/news_story.cfm?newsId=5052

[42] *Civil-Military Interoperability For GPS Assisted Aircraft Landings Demonstrated*
http://www.spacedaily.com/news/gps-01k.html

[43] *Raytheon conducts successful flight test of global positioning system (GPS) precision landing system*
http://www.raytheon.com/newsroom/briefs/022102.html

[44] *FedEx Express Selects Rockwell Collins Multi-Mode Receivers*
http://www.rockwellcollins.com/news/page2930.html

[45] *GLU-920 MMR Global Landing System*
http://www.rockwellcollins.com/ecat/AT/GLU-920.html?smenu=204

[46] *Anti-hijacking system operable in emergencies to deactivate on-board flight controls and remotely pilot aircraft utilizing autopilot*, United States Patent, Filed: October 9, 2001
http://patft.uspto.gov/netacgi/nph-Parser?Sect2=PTO1&Sect2=HITOFF&p=1&u=%2Fnetahtml%2FPTO%2Fsearch-bool.html&r=1&f=G&l=50&d=PALL&RefSrch=yes&Query=PN%2F6641087

[47] *Aircraft Communication Addressing and Reporting System*
http://en.wikipedia.org/wiki/ACARS

[48] *ARIES: NASA Langley's Airborne Research Facility*
http://www.cs.odu.edu/~mln/ltrs-pdfs/NASA-aiaa-2002-5822.pdf

[49] *Honeywell Aims To Test Crash—Evading System On Larger Planes*
http://www.aviationweek.com/aw/generic/story_generic.jsp?channel=aviationdaily&id=news/eva08133.xml

[50] *Airbus Shows Interest in Honeywell's Auto Pull-Up Software*
http://www.aviationweek.com/aw/generic/story_generic.jsp?channel=awst&id=news/09265p08.xml&headline=Airbus

[51] *FANS: Where Is It for Business Aviation?*
http://www.aviationweek.com/aw/generic/story_generic.jsp?channel=bca&id=news/FANS033.xml&headline=null&next=0

[52] *767 Flight Deck and Avionics—January 2002, Page 123*
http://www.smartcockpit.com/pdf/plane/boeing/B767/misc/0001/

[53] *757/767: Air Traffic Services Systems Requirements and Objectives—Generation 2*, Page 41 (Boeing, May 12, 2000)
http://www.boeing.com/commercial/caft/cwg/ats_dl/757-767_ATS_SRO.pdf

[54] *757/767: Air Traffic Services Systems Requirements and Objectives—Generation 2*, Page 41 (Boeing, May 12, 2000)
http://www.boeing.com/commercial/caft/cwg/ats_dl/757-767_ATS_SRO.pdf

[55] *757/767: Air Traffic Services Systems Requirements and Objectives—Generation 2*, Page 3 (Boeing, May 12, 2000)
http://www.boeing.com/commercial/caft/cwg/ats_dl/757-767_ATS_SRO.pdf

[56] *FANS Implementation in South Pacific* (June, 2001)
www.cena.fr/pages/1actu/atmrd/6lun18_06.pdf

[57] *757/767: Air Traffic Services Systems Requirements and Objectives—Generation 2*, Page 49 (Boeing, May 12, 2000)
http://www.boeing.com/commercial/caft/cwg/ats_dl/757-767_ATS_SRO.pdf

[58] *757/767: Air Traffic Services Systems Requirements and Objectives—Generation 2*, Page 50 (Boeing, May 12, 2000)
http://www.boeing.com/commercial/caft/cwg/ats_dl/757-767_ATS_SRO.pdf

[59] *757/767: Air Traffic Services Systems Requirements and Objectives—Generation 2*, Page 50 (Boeing, May 12, 2000)
http://www.boeing.com/commercial/caft/cwg/ats_dl/757-767_ATS_SRO.pdf

[60] *THE TWENTY-SEVENTH MEETING OF THE INFORMAL PACIFIC ATC COORDINATING GROUP* (November 2007)
http://www.faa.gov/about/office_org/ . . . /documents/IPACG/IPACG27/WP11_DAR . . .

[61] *Dilution of Precision (GPS)*
http://en.wikipedia.org/wiki/Dilution_of_precision_(GPS)

[62] *Dilution of Precision (GPS)*
http://en.wikipedia.org/wiki/Dilution_of_precision_(GPS)

[63] *Trimble's Planning Software*
http://www.trimble.com/abouttrimble.shtml

[64] *GPS ALMANACS/YUMA FOR YEAR 2001*
http://www.navcen.uscg.gov/?Do=gpsArchives&path=ALMANACS/YUMA&year=2001

[65] *NTSB Affirms Dubious Explanation For Pentagon "Black Box" Data File Time Stamp Discrepancy*
http://www.911blogger.com/node/18294

[66] *Was Essential 9/11 Aircraft 'Blackbox' Identification Information Withheld From NTSB?*
http://www.911blogger.com/node/16089

[67] *Flight Data Recorder Handbook for Aviation Accident Investigations*
http://www.ntsb.gov/Aviation/Manuals/FDR_Handbook.pdf

[68] *NTSB Elaborates On Absent Records Pertaining To Positively Identified 9/11 Aircraft Wreckage, Including 2 Flight Data Recorders*
http://www.911blogger.com/node/17139

[69] *Study of Autopilot, Navigation Equipment, and Fuel Consumption Activity Based on United Airlines Flight 93 and American Airlines Flight 77 Digital Flight Data Recorder Information*
http://www.ntsb.gov/info/autopilot_AA77_UA93_study.pdf

[70] *COMMISSION SENSITIVE UNCLASSIFIED—MEMORANDUM FOR THE RECORD—Interviews of United Airlines and American Airlines personnel in key roles on September 11, 2001*
http://media.nara.gov/9-11/MFR/t-0148-911MFR-01098.pdf

[71] *Another amazing coincidence related to the WTC*
http://www.911blogger.com/node/13272

[72] *Federal Building and Fire Safety Investigation of the World Trade Center Disaster: Passive Fire Protection*
http://wtc.nist.gov/NISTNCSTAR1-6A.pdf

[73] *World Trade Center Building Performance Study*
http://www.fema.gov/pdf/library/fema403_ch1.pdf

[74] *Airport Surveillance Radar*
http://www.faa.gov/air_traffic/technology/asr-11/

[75] *Fact Sheet—Host and Oceanic Computer System Replacement (HOCSR) Program*
http://www.faa.gov/news/fact_sheets/news_story.cfm?newsId=4950

[76] *September 11, 2001: Flight 175 Nearly Collides with Two Other Planes*
http://www.historycommons.org/context.jsp?item=a855nearcollision#a855nearcollision

[77] *A Sky Filled With Chaos, Uncertainty and True Heroism*
http://www.washingtonpost.com/ac2/wp-dyn?pagename=article&node=nation/specials/attacked&contentId=A41095-2001Sep16

[78] *Air Traffic Control: FAA Plans to Renlace Its Host Commuter System*
http://archive.gao.gov/paprpdf2/160369.pdf

[79] *COMMISSION SENSITIVE UNCLASSIFIED MEMORANDUM FOR THE RECORD: Interviews of United Airlines and American Airlines Personnel*
http://media.nara.gov/9-11/MFR/t-0148-911MFR-01098.pdf

[80] *The Post 9/11 Transponder*
http://www.aviationtoday.com/av/issue/feature/12731.html

[81] *Aviation Transponder Interrogation Modes*
http://en.wikipedia.org/wiki/Mode_S#Mode_S

[82] *Mode S Transponder—Incorrect Setting of ICAO 24-Bit Aircraft Address*
http://ad.easa.europa.eu/ad/2011-14

[83] *Mode S—Assignment of 24-bit Aircraft Addresses to State Aircraft*
http://www.eurocontrol.int/mil/public/standard_page/cns_sur_modes_24bAA.html

[84] *September 11, 2001: Reagan Airport Controllers Notified of Unidentified Aircraft Approaching Washington*
http://www.historycommons.org/context.jsp?item=a933reaganwarned#a933reaganwarned

[85] *The 9/11 Commission Report*, Page 9
http://www.9-11commission.gov/report/911Report.pdf

[86] *The 9/11 Commission Report*, Page 16
http://www.9-11commission.gov/report/911Report.pdf

[87] *The 9/11 Commission Report*, Page 18
http://www.9-11commission.gov/report/911Report.pdf

[88] *The 9/11 Commission Report*, Page 20
http://www.9-11commission.gov/report/911Report.pdf

[89] *The 9/11 Commission Report*, Page 25
http://www.9-11commission.gov/report/911Report.pdf

[90] *The 9/11 Commission Report*, Page 454
http://www.9-11commission.gov/report/911Report.pdf

[91] *'We have planes. Stay quiet'—Then silence*
http://www.guardian.co.uk/world/2001/oct/17/september11.usa

Chapter 5

[1] *UA 175's Mile Long 20 Degree Banked Turn On 9/11*
http://www.youtube.com/watch?v=FZi7TiXWcC4

[2] *Plausibility of 9/11 Aircraft Attacks Generated By GPS-Guided Aircraft Autopilot Systems*
http://www.journalof911studies.com/volume/2008/AutopilotSystemsMonaghan.pdf

[3] *NIST NCSTAR 1-5A* (PDF page 195)
http://wtc.nist.gov/NCSTAR1/PDF/NCSTAR%201-5A%20Ch%201-8.pdf

[4] *UA 175's Final 18 Degrees of Banking Turn*
http://www.youtube.com/watch?v=Kx8wYDNGRkk

[5] *In-flight Demonstrations of Curved Approaches and Missed Approaches in Mountainous Terrain*
http://waas.stanford.edu/~wwu/jennings/publications/ION98/iongps98.pdf

[6] *NIST NCSTAR 1-5A* (PDF page 124)
http://wtc.nist.gov/NCSTAR1/PDF/NCSTAR%201-5A%20Ch%201-8.pdf

[7]   *The Use of Land and Sea Based Wind Data in a Simple Circulation Model*
      http://journals.ametsoc.org/doi/abs/10.1175/1520-0485%281984%29014%3C0193%3ATUOLAS%3E2.0.CO%3B2

[8]   *NIST NCSTAR 1-5A* (PDF page 121)
      http://wtc.nist.gov/NCSTAR1/PDF/NCSTAR%201-5A%20Ch%201-8.pdf

[9]   *NIST NCSTAR 1-5A* (PDF page 157)
      http://wtc.nist.gov/NCSTAR1/PDF/NCSTAR%201-5A%20Ch%201-8.pdf

[10] *NIST NCSTAR 1-5A* (PDF page195)
      http://wtc.nist.gov/NCSTAR1/PDF/NCSTAR%201-5A%20Ch%201-8.pdf

[11] *Flight Operations Briefing Notes: Approach Techniques* (PDF page 3)
      http://www.mediafire.com/?2mn3hcymyig

[12] *Wind Triangle*
      http://en.wikipedia.org/wiki/Wind_triangl

[13] *9/11 Aircraft 'Black Box' Serial Numbers Mysteriously Absent*
      http://911blogger.com/news/2008-02-26/911-aircraft-black-box-serial-numbers-mysteriously-absent

[14] *Pentagon 9/11 Flight 'Black Box' Data File Created Before Actual 'Black Box' Was Recovered?*
      http://911blogger.com/news/2008-05-18/pentagon-911-flight-black-box-data-file-created-actual-black-box-was-recovered

[15] *767 Flight Deck and Avionics* (January, 2002, page 12)
      http://www.mediafire.com/?tm00rjyjcqy

[16] United Airlines Boeing 767-322 Flight Deck (February, 2002)
      http://www.airliners.net/photo/United-Airlines/Boeing-767-322-ER/0225641/L/&sid=abcabac05fbf4200bd53c1a562ca8dc8

[17] America Airlines Boeing 767-322 Flight Deck (November, 2000)
      http://www.airliners.net/photo/American-Airlines/Boeing-767-323-ER/0125435/L/&sid=a5531a1bana1/obdf16 9fae1230e7da8

[18] *Onboard Loadable Software*
      http://www.boeing.com/commercial/aeromagazine/aero_05/textonly/ps02txt.html

Chapter 6

[1]   *8:51 a.m. September 11, 2001: Last Radio Contact with Flight 77*
      http://www.historycommons.org/context.jsp?item=a850lastradio#a850lastradio

[2]   *9:05 am (and After) September 11, 2001: Flight 77 Reappears on Radar*
      http://www.historycommons.org/context.jsp?item=a905reappears#a905reappears

[3]   *(9:10 a.m.) September 11, 2001: Washington Flight Control Sees Unidentified Plane*
      http://www.historycommons.org/context.jsp?item=a910mysteryplane#a910mysteryplane

[4]   *The Pentacon - Eyewitnesses Speak, Conspiracy Revealed*
      http://www.thepentacon.com/

[5]   *Rapid Wall Breaching Kit (RWBK)*
      http://www.youtube.com/watch?v=wptjeH7sO9c

[6]   *Washington DC Fox Affiliate Captures 2nd Explosion At Pentagon On 9/11*
      http://www.youtube.com/watch?v=jSaOHne8FV4

[7]   *September 21, 2001: Report Suggests There Are Confiscated Videos of Pentagon Crash*
      http://www.historycommons.org/context.jsp?item=a092101missingvideos#a092101missingvideos

[8] *9:36 a.m.) September 11, 2001: Reagan Airport Control Tower Notified about Approaching Aircraft*
http://www.historycommons.org/context.jsp?item=a936towerwarned#a936towerwarned

[9] *Pentagon Building Performance Report*
http://www.asce.org/Product.aspx?id=2147485891

Chapter 7

[1] *Pentagon says it has no records of bin Laden's death; CIA hasn't answered open records request*
http://www.therepublic.com/view/story/ec15acc54eed444fb76d9c15c7eaf8f9/US—Sunshine-Week-Bin-Laden

[2] *Government could hide existence of records under FOIA rule proposal*
http://www.syracuse.com/news/index.ssf/2011/10/government_could_hide_existenc.html